I *am* Cyprus

Armida Publications is a member of the Independent Publishers Guild (UK), and a member of the Independent Book Publishers Association (USA)

www.armidabooks.com | Great Literature. One Book At A Time.

Summary:

"You are not Cypriot." But I tell them I am. Cyprus is all I have ever known.

What is a Cypriot? Too often the story told of Cyprus makes the island nation seem dully monocultural, or bicultural at best. Yet the life stories Annetta Benzar has collected and retold here celebrate a country that is full of diversity, and in which there is a tale from a different part of the world around every corner. In these pages you will read stories of blood, stories of borders and border-crossings, stories of brides, of fathers, footballers, fear and fate, told by an eclectic cast connected to countries as separate as the United States, the Philippines, the Congo or the Crimea.

As they reflect on the sometimes heartbreaking, sometimes inspiring and sometimes funny experience of living in Cyprus, Annetta Benzar, herself a Cypriot citizen of Belarussian origin, weaves the stories together to form a portrait of a dynamic and fascinating country.

[1. SOCIAL SCIENCE / Emigration & Immigration, 2. SOCIAL SCIENCE / Discrimination,
3. SOCIAL SCIENCE / Human Geography, 4. SOCIAL SCIENCE / Refugees,
5. SOCIAL SCIENCE / Anthropology / Cultural & Social,
6. BIOGRAPHY & AUTOBIOGRAPHY / Survival]

In collaboration with
European University Cyprus

Cover Photographs from Unsplash

Disclaimer:
The views and opinions expressed in this book are those of the individuals featured and do not necessarily reflect the opinions of the Author or the Publisher.

1st edition: November 2020

ISBN-13 (paperback): 978-9925-573-22-6

I *am* Cyprus

25 Stories of the migrant
and refugee experience in Cyprus

ANNETTA
BENZAR

ARMIDA

TABLE OF CONTENTS

INTRODUCTION

I grew up in Cyprus. Some of the most vivid memories from those early years, besides being dragged (in full tantrum mode) to the beach every day from May to October, revolve around a 'door'. My grandmother, as so many others in our neighbourhood, preferred to leave our front door wide open. This was not a habit she had practiced back in Belarus. There, our doors had two sets of locks that each bragged about their own sets of clicking and grinding sounds, a one two three and a one, two. Closed. I knew that sound. But I never paid it as much attention or thought as when we moved across land and sea to a house where grandmother thought it inappropriate to lock. I used to think it was because she always wanted to be the first to see and know what was going on outside (possibly one of her grandchildren getting up to mischief) or so she could be prepared for this unfamiliar outside world walking into her own. My grandmother, or babushka as I call her, is the kind who doesn't enjoy surprises. Nor did she ever expect anything out of the ordinary to occur in that sleepy part of the island we used to call home. I don't remember ever seeing my grandparents lock up our first house in Cyprus even on the rare occasion when the whole family left the premises. The only keys I recall ever seeing them carry were for the car. *Why should we lock the doors?* They would say. *It's such a pain to go through the whole process of opening it up again. We are in Cyprus now.* Everyone was welcome, in their eyes, and there was never any point in trying to keep anyone out. In those days, we used to have many visitors arriving for a cup of tea and draniki, to stay for lunch or for the whole summer break. There was always someone coming in and out of that open door and, however much my mother complained about the dust or dirt flying in from the fields surrounding our house, my grandmother was adamant in keeping that door open. Sun or rain. Sometimes even at night.

In her own way, babyshka was trying to become what she believed was a 'Cypriot'. During her time on the island, she was never able to grasp the local language other than the basics ('geia sou,' 'gala,' 'psomi'[1]). Instead, she held onto a different form of communication. My babyshka talked hospitality. She opened her doors because that is what she had read defined the island in the brochure she was given before the whole family uprooted their lives in Minsk, Belarus, and emigrated to this tiny island in the middle of the Mediterranean. She believed the way to her neighbours' hearts was in adopting their habits and their character. Her talk was her act ...the less words she felt she needed... and the more she acted the less words she was able to grasp year in and year out.

In many ways, that was our experience of the island. Our neighbours' doors remained open and a glimpse of their life inside was always visible if you were to walk by. As if you were part of the going-ons inside their home. But as the years went by, I began to feel uneasy about the doors ...I felt the outsideness. The vulnerability the threat of an open door signified. Was my neighbour watching as I walked by? Were they waiting for me to walk up the steps to the porch, my foot cross the door sill and, at that very moment, be hit back

---

1 'hello', 'milk', 'bread'

with the door, closing, A click. A rattling sound. Without a word of warning. Almost a threat. Watching us walk by. Sometimes I wondered whether the doors remained open just so our hosts can push us back out. Quickly. Without a word of warning.

Cyprus' history can be described as an unintentional open door. In its 10,000 years of recorded history, it has been occupied and colonised for longer than it has been a sovereign independent state. The Achaeans, the Phoenicians, the Assyrians, the Egyptians, the Persians, the Romans, the English, the Lusignans, the Venetians, the Ottomans. Even today, it remains an island divided between Greek-Cypriots in the South and Turkish-Cypriots in the North as a consequence of the 1974 invasion. The island's mixed history is reflected in its buildings, many of them exposed to the public eye. From its Neolithic archaeological sites and the Venetian Walls surrounding the Old City of Nicosia, to the Islamic Mosques and the Roman monasteries.

The island has become a witness to a fluidity of migration of people offering their own history to the island. Though they were once uncertain, the wave-like motion with which they arrived has transformed into a soil in which they strive to grow their roots. So we as current residents, fellow island sharers, experience a different Cypriot geography. Yet, how different is the Cypriot landscape today compared to that of twenty, thirty years ago. Limassol with its towering luxury apartment buildings that are plastered with 'продается' banners taking up more space than the road signs. The numerous Asian stores where locals go to buy their rice noodles and tofu, their spices and rice. That one street in the old town of Nicosia that has at least seven barber shops, all with Arabic signs and on another that Armenian quick stop that is always crowded on a Friday or Saturday night with people waiting for some shawarma before drinks. The active mosques. Kofinou Camp. The Red Lanterns for Chinese New Year hanging by the neighbours' front doors. The annual Russian-Cyprus Festival, SeptemberFest, the Phillipine Cook-Offs, the Sri Lankan dancers at the annual Spring Festival, belly dancers, the school children gliding between Greek and Russian, Greek and English, Greek and Filipino, Greek and German, Swedish, Hebrew, Romanian, Spanish, Bulgarian, Arabic, Persian, French...

'Well, he doesn't look very Cypriot!'

This was the comment circulating both online and offline when Marios Georgiou competed as part of the Cypriot Gymnastics Team at the 2018 Commonwealth Games. Despite articles stating the fact that the gymnast had a Greek-Cypriot father, it was not until he had won the medals for the island, did the comments move away from a debate over his origins and, therefore, the legitimacy of his belonging to the Cypriot Team (his features reflect his Filipino heritage) to pride for the national flag being displayed abroad. This comment is reminiscent of those made in the early 90s about the job openings for 'cabaret dancers' (I place this in quotation marks because, in most cases, the job description implied though did not state outright duties that were more than just dancing).

A double face. "Come," they would say, "come be part of the new island." But only if you stay within your own doors. Not for Cypriot girls.

Part of the Cypriot community the doors were open for a short while. As long as they performed, they could remain in the house. Not as part of the family but as a constant outsider, someone who would never be accepted as part of the Cypriot community. The door was and is always ready for the 'foreigner' to return 'back to where you came from'.

Memory has become a battlefield. We no longer fight with swords but stories. The stories we choose to hear and believe, lead us to fundamentally align with the narrative's ideology. Slowly, the stories form a history that is repeated, generation after generation, and a nationalism that is bred into its citizens. This is true of Cyprus. The unjust treatment of asylum seekers, refugees and migrant workers is constantly being exposed by local media and by groups who work closely with these communities. Yet, these stories are soon lost, forgotten, burned to the ground and buried in the soil. Left in suitcases at the bottom of a lake. There is rarely a memorial for them. It is as if they had never shared the island, never left an imprint on its greater narrative. This inhumane treatment of the 'outsider', however, is also true of the larger European family of nations, especially in the wake of the 'refugee crisis'. The stories we choose to hear and repeat will determine the development of the European narrative. Most importantly, in the face of current hostility towards refugees from the Middle East and Africa, these stories will define the future of the European Union as it passes through its own mid-life crisis. Who are Europeans, ask Nevena Nancheva and Timofey Agarin in *A European Crisis: Perspectives on Refugees, Solidarity and Europe*, and with whom do they hold solidarity? The interstate freedom of movement under the Schengen agreement that was once a proud cornerstone of the EU is now being characterised as its curse in political discourse. The safeguarding of human rights and high standard of protection for refugees and asylum seekers is no longer a priority. Indeed, states are not even willing to undertake their basic responsibilities under the Dublin treaties. Instead, the European Union is slowly closing its borders. We can even say, its doors.

The purpose of this collection is to shed light on how

many stories from 'outsiders' have helped build the political and social makeup of the island and how the island has in turn treated them. The 'alien', the 'foreigner', the 'enemy', the 'immigrant', the 'migrant', the 'refugee'. The beautician, the driver, the business partner, the student. The neighbour, the daughter-in-law. The child. The one who knocked on the door. The former 'guest' who has now built a home. Their stories are changing the landscape of the island and it is time their contribution is acknowledged. Their solidarity and their belonging, their Cypriotness and their Cyprus. It is all one. History.

NOTES

The following stories were collected between 2017 and 2018. Any identifying information (such as names, age etc.) have been altered to protect the privacy of the individuals. Most of the stories were written in collaboration with their protagonists and are all truthful according to their memory. The stories have not been fact-checked and the opinions remain those of the storytellers themselves.

Blood

I am DEVRIM

Today I have two languages that barely add up to one.

BREAK DOWN

'I'll tell you an anecdote.'

April. We are sitting outside a kafeneio on rickety chairs, at times rocking back to discern faces in the passing crowd. Devrim sits opposite me, greeting person after person with genuine warmth, name by name, almost a crowd. He is small, slightly hunched with a mix of soft abruptness in the way he lets every word walk or cascade over his tongue and out of his lips. At first, his voice had taken me by surprise. Low, a rising murmur, never whipped into speed, a hum of endurance. There was something in the way he would pause as if to contemplate over the consequences his words may or may not have, as though by giving them up freely he would lose or gain a piece of himself or maybe a piece that was not yet him, but could be.

We sat maneuvering through generic topics for a while that trailed into discussions on the theoretical scholarship of Bhabha, Anderson and Spivak, reminiscing over past lectures, over first readings, over their conclusions. Then, slowly, naturally, we drifted into the more personal.

DIVISION

He tells me he is divided, or at least inhabits multiple

hyphens. Turkish-Cypriot. British-Cypriot. British-Turkish-Cypriot? I search for these hyphens on his arms, as if they could be branded into his skin, part of its pigmentation. He is a child of Turkish-Cypriots parents, and I can't help but compare him to the Greek-Cypriots playing tavli on the nearby table. How stark is this dividing line through Nicosia, how sharp does it enter the genes of the people on either side, who live within and without its borders? I come up with very little. Even Devrim's hand gestures accenting his words, appear to match theirs, playing a game of mirrors. What divides this Turkish-Cypriot from his Greek-Cypriot counterpart? He laughs at my question. For one, Devrim points out, he doesn't speak Greek but Turkish, or Turkish-Cypriot. But other than that, he shrugs and relates an anecdote from his primary school days in the North.

'One day my brother came home and asked what the Greek-Cypriots looked like.

And my mum was like, "What do you mean?"

"What do they look like?"

Because what he was taught at school was that they were monsters and my mum had to explain no no they are human beings and unfortunately that was the image most people had of the other. I remember one day when I started to cross to the South, when the boundaries opened, I was asked like, "What do you live in?" and I was like, "What kind of question is that?" They said, "We live in houses. What about you?" I was like, "What do you think other people live in, caves?" Because, unfortunately, their education system has instilled the idea that we are barbaric.'

The creatures of the other side are no longer mysteries to him, ever since the border opened in 2003. He not only crossed and observed but has made the decision to live on the 'other' side of the Ledra crossing, among the villains of his school history books. From his room on the Southern part of the Old City, you can almost see the mosques nestled behind the police-controlled checkpoint. His mother was born in the South, he tells me. And her mother before her. He is Turkish-Cypriot, but he is not bound to the North, he will not be. This is where he belongs, he insists, this part is home.

LABYRINTH

Within these Venetian walls lies the Old City. Here you will find the perspiration of enthusiastic tourists, the heavy brows of straining migrant workers and the light dampness of street musicians scrambling along the labyrinth of streets under the blaze of the sun. The Old City leads you to lose you, down side streets crossed with graffitied Holy Mary's gaping at passerbys, bell tolls ringing from St Sophia's minaret in protest against the voices from the local market, road signals pointing in every direction, south, north, 'Stop', 'No Entry'. Stone houses mingle like the men in the coffeeshops with their balconies reaching out to hold hands, or to press an ear against their neighbor's wall. All the better to hear the 'kirioi' and 'kiries', the men and women, across the narrow streets, collecting gossip like years. Now their mouths are being covered with posters. Like silence. Like the awaited.

'Break Down the Wall!' the prints demand. *Open the last divided city in Europe.*

GAMES

Age: 0-2 Cyprus (North)
Age: 2-7 UK

Age: 7-13 Cyprus (North)
Age: 13-18 UK
Age: 18+ Cyprus/UK/Cyprus/UK/Cyprus/UK/Cyprus

Upon having emigrated (for the second time) to the UK, Devrim's parents insisted their two sons switch over to using English exclusively. At 13, other than the little he had picked up at public school back in Cyprus, Devrim's supply of English was little at best. It is no surprise, therefore, that that particular decision of his parents had not been favourably welcomed. No Turkish at home had meant much more than not speaking Turkish, it had meant TV with no Turkish channels, no dubs, no subtitles, no books, original or translated into Turkish, not even complaining against house chores in the familair 'Kıbrıs Türkçesi' dialect. Everything was in English. A new border had entered their home.

It is for the best, Devrim's parents had said or thought, it is not a punishment.

Think of it like a game, they had said. And they made it so. A game of mathematics, a game of economics, a game of winning and losing. A game of real life.

'Whoever uses a Turkish word while they are speaking, they have to put a penny into their jar. When it is full, you will get a book in English. So that is what started us in the short period. But she (my mother) realised she was not going to be able to beat us. After a while, my brother started to speak only in English and he forgot the Turkish language altogether. My parents were also caught out speaking Turkish. Whenever they would speak together in Turkish, my brother would say, "Ok you said this. That is 20 words, you owe 20p in the jar."'

That is how Devrim learnt English. Or thereabouts. He

is humble about his language or languages. The moves here and there, summers spent on the Mediterranean island, term time back in the cool of London, a Giorgos here and a George there, all took a toll, or so he says.

'Today,' he jokes, *'I have two languages that barely add up to one.'*

His thoughts, he tells me, are also mixed. A touch of Kibris, a curse in English, an affectionate sentiment, a retort, an apology. Within his body, the elements of language kiss, folding themselves into hugs, grasping at each other's arms. When turning to his friend, another fellow Turkish-Cypriot, to ask for clarification of an event, he flows from Kibris to English without missing a beat.

At his transition, the eyes from the nearby table glance up from their dice game. Their eyes watch him, curious (maybe), thinking (maybe), ears attempting to follow, *what did he say*? Turning back to me, Devrim transitions back to English. They who had been watching him also turn back. Their game continues.

MODERN VAMPIRE

'I am thalassemic by nature, meaning ever since from the age of 2 or 3 I have had to go to the hospital and take 2 or 3 units of blood.'

The taking, the giving, the pricking of the needle and the flow of the foreigner into his veins. His body no more partakes than becomes the space in which relations begin and end, or mingle. Devrim laughs, calling himself a vampire,

'A modern vampire, because I have donors for my blood hunger. I go to a clinic and they feed us there. I make jokes about it as well, because it is a lifelong condition.'

Each donor is anonymous; he has never met those who are within him. But he feels them, as they enter and take temporary siege along his veins. Pumping him with their own administration and systems, greed and hunger. n. As a counter-attack he is forced to prick himself, '12 hours-24 hours- sometimes even 36 hours' against the coloniser's excess of metal, of iron.

There is a shyness about him as he reflexively rubs the arm that had, only a few minutes before, been hit with Deferoxamine. It is clear he hadn't intended to mention his condition but, in attempting to express his attachment to the South, he couldn't ignore the health motives. Since childhood, he has been a patient at *The Thalassaemia Centre* in Nicosia, and living close by on the South side, is vital for maintaining his wellbeing. '*I am an outsider wherever I go,*' he murmurs, in that idiosyncratic way he has, that presumes words do not matter until they do. Humour that borders between laughter and tight lips. Like a joke taken out of context.

'So maybe the whole idea with the health situation helps because ever since I've known myself I can see that with blood it's something we can only get from donations from other people. When you look at blood, it's the same kind of blood. There is no blue blood, or black blood, or white blood. It's just one kind of blood.'

There is a breeze from the North that makes me slightly shiver. Shiver as I nod with him. Us both shivering and nodding at it all, at this joke that is as serious as they come.

REVOLUTION

'I'll tell you an anecdote.

There was a period that I was doing some stencils. I did them mostly in the North. But I also did the same stencils in the South close to the borders with soldiers, instead of holding guns and bazookas, they were holding pink dildos. HUGE PINK DILDOS!'

A pause, a smirk and a sly chuckle.

'And I did this around the Old City. Both in the North and South. And when I was doing it in the South two friends of mine said, "Ok we have something as well, let's get together," and we formed this group to just go out and just color things.'

He would later send me photos of his work, apologetic for the quality of both the photo and the print itself, being a prototype, an idea just taking shape. The pink is rude, robbing attention from the dark outlines of the military men. It manifests in crudeness and violence, in absurdity, in a humor that sends me into long blasts of laughter.

'At one point when we were doing the stencil in the South, three guys approached us and asked us about what we were doing.

"Oh, just stencil, this and that, you know."

And they got really, really upset with the stencil of the soldier holding a pink dildo. Then they started to ask us where we are from, so my friend said,

"Well I am from here, I am half English and half Greek Cypriot, my friend is Turkish-Cypriot (pointing at me) and my other friend is Greek-Cypriot as well."

The response kind of shocked us all because it was like he started to shout.

"You are not Cypriot. Because you're a bastard (pointing at my Greek-Cypriot friend), you are half English and half Cypriot, therefore you are not true blood. And he is Turkish-Cypriot (pointing at me) so he is not Cypriot at all and she (they turned to our last friend) is only a woman."'

Pause. Why does he stop there? There is a revolution within him, bubbling. An attack of art, an art unapologetic but an art that doesn't take scraps, that throws those scraps back. That full stop almost seems stagnant, just a joke. I want it to be so much more.

'What is a Cypriot?' I ask him. There it is again, his smile. And an ending. With the curve of his mouth widening to show his teeth.

'*Bastards,*' he declares, and he raises the word to include all of us sitting there in the café, mingling around the Old City, painting the whole island in its pink glow, and his laugh echoes around us all.

I am ALEC

This is my life and
all I can tell you is this story.

Unity entails breakage. You can only make whole what was once unwhole, unite what was once merely units scattered like dust, fractions that were reaching and hoping to become that one thing: united. In archaeology, it is the breakages, the cracks, the points of departure where narratives begin. And unity can only hold its own stories if it had experienced seeing its own disassembled selves, lying on the floor, surrounded by darkness, and thinking, can I ever pick myself up from here?

'This is my life and all I can tell you is this story.'

Alec's adventures in Cyprus began in the summer of 2011 as part of an archaeological team excavating historic sites on the island. He had leaped at the offer of leaving the sleepy town in which he had grown up in back in the States.

'I was like, "Let's go and explore something different." So, I got home and I showed where Cyprus was on the map to my mom and her first response was, "Oh that's awful close to the Middle East." My response was, "Wow it's even further away than I thought it was! That's amazing I can't wait to go."'

His job was photographing the finds of the team as they dug into the history of the island. Through his lens, Alec explored the remains of Ancient Cyprus, one photograph at a time. He knew little of Cyprus before his arrival, and his curiosity from behind the lens soon took on new angles. He turned his eye towards a more contemporary scene.

'I was really interested in finding out how other gay people live. Since this was a place that really interested me from a geographic, archaeological, historical standpoint and this was a topic of interest I was working on at the time, I thought let's try to meet other people here. So, I downloaded Grindr and started to meet people, started to photograph and take their portraits as well. One of the things that always concerned me in my photographic practices is this power dynamic that happens between the photographer and subject. I go to this place, I take the photos, the primary word of concern for me is the word "take". I also wanted in some way to change that…I was wondering, how can I give back? How can I equalize that power dynamic? I started asking people, what is your life like here? I really wanted to know. A lot of what I was finding out was a lot of different types of religious, social, familial lives of people here, people staying relatively in the closet. There is so much fear coming out as a gay person here. Cyprus only had its first Gay Pride in 2014. And even then, there was a protest by the Church, an anti-gay protest. Everybody that I had spoken to, who I knew was gay, was very afraid. And so was I. The repercussions and punishments were always at the back of my mind.'

After his second summer spent in Cyprus, Alec received news that would alter the trajectory of his life. He was diagnosed with HIV.

'The doctor I was working with at the time went and chased through my history of partners and also based on the time the symptoms started to show up, we determined that I had contracted it here in Cyprus. At the time, I was applying to graduate school. All I could think about was, "Oh my god, this is a death sentence. I'm gonna die. This is the end of my life."'

The wholeness he had come to believe was his life was being ripped into pieces, the glue shadows of a future he didn't understand. But the fear of remaining unwhole, lying on the ground in the shadows for the rest of his life, caused more fear than picking up the pieces left of himself. The fear pushed him to a re-education, a re-adjusting, a re-imagining a life with HIV.

'I began educating myself, reading all I could about the diagnosis. With today's progress in medicine, it was soon clear it was not the death sentence I had written myself under. You take a pill. You are able to suppress the virus loading the body on the technical level to the point where you can't even transmit it to other people. It doesn't have an impact on your life expectancy anymore. It's a chronic condition but it's become as manageable as high blood pressure. Luckily, I was in New York where it is more socially accepted. You are seen as uneducated if you don't know about the latest developments.'

Fortunately for him, the crisis of reveling in the cracks was short-lived. It was a journey relearning who he was and what his body was enduring at that point, questions began to arise as to the source of his cracking: the encounter in Cyprus. Did the other guy know? If not, why not? Why wasn't he getting tested?

'So, the first time I came back after the diagnosis was in 2013, in the winter. I went back to the place where I had that encounter with that person. I wanted to understand what I felt about that place and person. I was not trying to find him…maybe subconsciously I was. He was not there. But then I also started to meet more people and really started to get a sense of what it's like to live in this community. What's it's like to live with this pressure, the familiar social factors, the legal hindrances? The power of the Church in Cyprus that plays a major role in the freedom of people and their expression of their sexuality? It's a really small community. There's a lot of stigma to being gay. Add HIV on top of that, and the outdated misinformation about HIV creates a lot of that suppression. So, I feel like in some ways visibility

is the best thing. Those suffering from HIV are afraid to visit the specific clinic that treats HIV because of the possibility of being seen and then people will start talking about them. Gossip is the thing here that is unlike anything I have ever seen. It really works to the disadvantage of everybody. It destroys lives, almost to the point of death. Physical death. There are issues with nurses being up to-date with how they treat people with HIV. I talked with someone recently, someone who visited a doctor here, who had the courage to. And what do they get for their efforts? This was last year now. This person said, "I have HIV", and the doctor got up and walked out of the room. Can you believe that? In Cyprus, the mindset is still stuck in the late 80s or 90s when was a death sentence. Even in medical circles. I am trying to change this by working with an NGO, educating the public about what it actually means to live with HIV. Not just as a lecture but in living out my words, being a model, in a sense, for the eyes of the public. I hope I have achieved that but in order to fully gain that position, I need to be here.

I'm trying to find a way to live here on a more permanent basis, so I can continue my work. For the past three years, I've been trying to find a way through employment to come here. But one of the major problems is that Cyprus will not allow a person with HIV outside of the EU to reside here on a long-term basis. In order for me to get a long-term residency permit I have to submit medical documentation that says I'm HIV negative, negative Hepatitis, Syphilis and Tuberculosis. I don't have that proof because I'm HIV Positive. If you come from outside of the EU, you have no choice but to go through the test unless you are a high ranking official of an international company, which I'm not. Or, the other option, is through family reunification. You are exempt from being asked from medical checks if you are being invited to the island as a family member or a spouse.

A friend, who is Cypriot, and who used to be my boyfriend but we are in a different relationship now, offered to marry me for family reunification. I sat on the offer for two and a half years trying to find some other way to do it and there is no other way. We're not together in that sort of sense anymore. But we have remained incredibly good friends… We're on the same page of what this means. What the responsibilities are for each of us. What romantically it means, essentially it means nothing, but it's not really what our relationship is about. He's one of my closest friends and the way that I see it is it's two people that are helping each other get what they want in the world. He wants me to be able to come here and do the work I am passionate about. I also want him to be able to go elsewhere and do the work that he wants to do too. The Parliament voted to allow civil unions in December of 2015 and it came into effect in the beginning of 2016. With civil unions, you don't have to have it published in a newspaper, you don't have to have a religious ceremony. It's just you go to the office, sign the documents, they give you a certificate that you are now in a civil union. It is quick and simple and we can stop there but that's not gonna stop us from having a little party though. It is an exciting new chapter for my life.

Of course, he only recently came out to his mother. He never told her when we were in a relationship, although I think she guessed at it. It was the summer and I was in short shorts…she must have assumed something was going on. And then he told her of his plans for the union and the reasons behind them. I was there. It was not a pleasant conversation.

His mother went, "That person was in my house! He was eating off my plates. You now have AIDS and my family is going to have AIDS!" And it turned into this whole big dramatic thing, which is weird now. I'm afraid to go back to his house now. She thinks I'm going to give them all AIDS (again). There was this bad relationship between mother and son that turned into this good relationship, which has now turned into this bad relationship. I am hoping it will change.

He's a strong person. He doesn't let these things stop him from what it is he's going to do that he knows is right, and he's not afraid to tell his family exactly how it is. This is why I'm doing it. These are my reasons for doing it and this is why I think it's right. For me this whole experience, being beside him, through it, it's been very instructive because it is, in a way, my intimate connection to the way the family unit works in Cyprus. The way it works when somebody is gay. The cultural attitudes. The more traditional attitudes. Easier to see and be immersed in firsthand experience. It's what I want. I don't want to be on the sidelines and speculate. I want to assimilate. What is this experience actually like? I'm never going to have that experience to the fullest that anyone who is born here or grew up here does. But I feel like one of the things that has been really important for me is the more I come back, the more I invest, the more that side of it is open to me. There is good and there is bad with it too. I don't know, I'm reluctant to say that I've become accepted but the more that people get used to having me being around… those barriers they start to go down. Which is not something would ever happen. It's special to me. I try not to take it for granted.

It is funny. Even though I came over here to photograph, to be behind the lens, my time here has forced me to come out from behind the camera and into the spotlight. To become visible. And, I don't want to say subjects but yes subjects, they are coming out from the scenery and reaching out, they are the ones with the eye, watching me. We are clasping hands between frames, between the limits of the photograph, the landscape and the visual. By sharing our experiences, the gay scene is changing in Cyprus and I am so grateful to be part of that. I feel fulfilled being part of that and this is why I want to become a part of Cyprus.

When I first came to Cyprus and I was photographing these archaeological remains. I had a part of the statue on my coffee stand to photograph and, as I was turning around, I bumped the coffee stand. The whole thing fell apart like into pieces right there. I freaked out like, "Oh my God, I've just broken a priceless antiquity. It was an accident but they're gonna send me to jail. I'm never going to see my family again. Blah blah blah." I locked myself in the lab for 30 minutes, just crying.

Then I went to the archaeologist and said, "Something happened, I don't know what to do. I'm really freaking out." So, they went and looked at it and said, 'Oh don't worry. It was broken before. We'll glue it back together tomorrow.'"

For me, that statue has become the metaphor for my life and relationship to Cyprus. There is this object that is whole and then by happenstance there is this accident. The thing crumbles but then you can put it back together again. Sometimes the bricks can tell you something how the object was destroyed and when it was destroyed. In what manner and for what reason it was destroyed by looking at how it was broken. So, in a way it's this symbol of destruction but also of rebirth, having memories about that destruction, as well, and what you do with that destruction coming forward.'

The cracks reform the piece, exactly as it was, and, simultaneously, as it has never been. For Alec, his cracks have brought him to a place where he can help glue others back together. Out of the darkness and into the light.

I am NILÜFER

The mind and the island
share the same imprisonment.

Fairytales never go out of fashion, happily ever-afters do. There are tales of princes, and fairies and witches, and love. The following story is about finding love but not a happily ever after; about seeing what is real and what is imagined and choosing both. It is about girl meets heartache and disenchantment, it is about girl meets witch, and girl turns back to see all the magic that she could have grasped had she only…let it be. A young woman, a blue-haired spirit, a believer of darkness and light, in the inscriptions upon hands, a writer with a wand who can cast spells merely with the worlds she creates for her heroes. She is a creatress, a mother to the stories of the women in her care. She appeares out of times of surprise and unfamiliarity, like the Pied Piper with his fiddle, swaying in bright blue leggings and purple pashminas, clasping her metal water bottle in one hand and a thumb, erect, to catch whatever adventure that may be passing her way. Aurora (let's call her Aurora) dances like a trickster to music but her smile radiates sincerity, compassion; she is restless and hurt, she is powerful and loud, she is small and searching. She is everything, like a stranger to no place.

But Aurora is not the protagonist here, Nilüfer is. For Nilüfer the magic that she had once believed in, the magical spell of Cyprus had lost its vitality, its fluorescent colours. Maybe it began with the stories of her grandparents, her 'dede' and 'anneanne', about the fall of their own life and dreams at the breakout of the civil war in 1974.

'I grew up listening to my grandparents' stories of Larnaca, what life was like there before and after the 60s. My grandfather was born in Larnaca, in 1921, to a family who were born and raised there. My mother was born in Arabahmet, Nicosia, but her eldest siblings were born in Larnaca. I naturally start talking about my mother's parents as "my grandparents", for my grandparents on my dad's side passed away shortly after I was born. I think they were originally from a village where my father was born, Avdimou, a village near Limassol. My father's father used to own a bar in Avdimou, where Cypriots and English soldiers used to hang out a lot. I know that my dad used to go there to help his dad when he was a kid.

What I heard from my grandfather is that Cypriots, Greek and Turkish, worked and lived together, something very difficult to imagine for me; to have a blend of one Cypriot culture; one Cypriot culture until the conflicts began in the 60s until the invasion in 1974. Especially before 1963, and even before 1974, you couldn't say that there was a division like we have today.

My grandfather is probably the oldest person now, who was born and raised in Larnaca. He started working for a shoemaker when he was about thirteen/fourteen. He learnt everything about shoemaking from a Greek Cypriot man. My grandfather became the most famous shoemaker, "kunduracı" as we call it, of Larnaca. There weren't many anyway. When he was old enough and earning money, he bought a place, created an atelier for himself, and worked with Greek and Turkish Cypriots in his studio; designing, making shoes. When the conflicts broke out in the 60s, he had to leave his studio and bought a shop in the Turkish territory and he started selling fabricated shoes. He couldn't continue to work as a shoemaker, for his studio and his tools were left be-

hind, in the Greek territory. It was difficult to stay there as many incidents started taking place.

1974 is marked by the Turkish Invasion of Cyprus. We were taught at school that this was the "Cyprus Peace Operation". The same operation took place in Afrin recently, remember? Most Turkish Cypriots and the Turks who live in Cyprus celebrate it, even now. They start a night watch on the 19th of July and the celebrations continue to the 20th with jets whizzing in the air, cutting the sky into two. It's a night watch until sunrise, and an act of militarist, separatist emotions in my opinion. In 1974, the Turkish army approached the shores of Kyrenia, and the Greek Cypriots who lived in the north moved to southern parts of the island. A group of political people gathered at that time that included Denktaş, who told the Turkish Cypriots who were still in South Cyprus, to leave everything behind, and that they should move to the north. They were told that they would get new homes, new properties. This is when the division really happened. My mum tells me that the Greek police or the army never told anyone to leave; her grandfather and her youngest aunt stayed in the south for a while, but then moved to Famagusta. It wasn't a matter of safety only; it was also because their families and friends had moved to other places in the northern territory already. Most people were left alone if they chose to stay where they belonged. It was a time of conflict and chaos between 1963 and 1974; everyone killing each other, Turks and Greeks, and the political organisations had been murdering those who spread opposing ideas against division. One of my uncles was arrested during the war in 1974; he was imprisoned for three months and when he was finally released he left the country and moved to the UK when he was sixteen. He wasn't tortured or starved like many others in prison. He didn't suffer like many other Cypriots did.

My mother grew up in a house that paralleled Finikoudes beach. She and my grandfather tell me that in the summer my grandfather used to take his six children and went to Mackenzie beach. He taught them how to swim, and they all love the sea. Mum always tells me that it's very difficult for her to live in a city where she cannot see the sea. Perhaps that is why I love it there, to be in the waters of Larnaca. It's their memories of Larnaca and my Cypriot skin covered in Larnaca sand. The sea is shallow and there is nothing special about it. But it's the most beautiful place to me.

They left Larnaca and everything they owned behind, and were given a house in Ayorgi, Kyrenia, and some land, where our house is now. This exchange that happened wasn't legit or anything, many people lost property at that time, and some got very rich. Some got keys to hotels, large amounts of land, and so on. They call it the era of "ganimet" in Cyprus.

My nan tells me that when they moved into the house in Ayorgi, it was a mess. There were still pots and pans in the kitchen that contained half-cooked food. The people (who had left the house) rushed to escape for their lives, not to get killed or arrested by the Turkish army.

When they were going to leave Larnaca and move to this new house, they had to get permission from the police. At that time, my grandfather had a Greek friend who helped them out with this, and they managed to make a deal with a Greek taxi owner who drove them to the North. They only took some clothes and that was it. My nan used to work as a tailor and she had to leave her sewing machine, materials... They just turned up somewhere they knew nothing about, nothing familiar, and desolate; nothing in their hands to support themselves with. My nan told me how they found mattresses, tables, chairs etc. from the houses that were abandoned. The table that they still have in their house is a large wooden table, a Cypriot one. Most of the Cypriots have the same table in their kitchens or living rooms. They started getting sorted slowly. But the time after the war was desperate; there was no sense of belonging and nothing familiar. They just had to deal with this, on their own. Basically, every moment was fought for survival. How they survived with six children…I don't know. And without the government's help. What help? I learnt through these stories that governments, political figuresnever cared about Cypriots, especially then.'

Faith in the government dissipated early in Nilüfer. Its abandonment of her grandparents, and all its people, at a time they needed it most, broke whatever hope or trust she may have had in its goodness, in its authenticity. When her grandparents had nothing to give, closed doors were all they received. Nothing can come of nothing. And nothing could hold Nilüfer's loyalty for a face turned. Magic turned to dust.

Instead, Nilüfer sought magic in her parents' lives. In their resistance.

'They both left Cyprus to study in Turkey in late 70s-early 80s. My mum was studying finance and my dad was in med school. I think it was the first day of school that my mum saw my dad. He was in a khaki jacket, thick eyelashes covering hazel eyes. He looked very serious she says. They became friends, started going out, and were engaged for 8 years, for my dad had to finish school before they got married. They were both members of left-wing unions that supported communism during the upheaval of politics in Turkey. The 80s was a really dramatic time because the police could arrest you on the streets if you didn't carry your ID. Everyone had the potential of being a suspect at that time; it was very risky to be a member of a leftist union or a leftist party. There were a lot of protests going on and my father, a poor student and an activist at that time, got in trouble several times for painting slogans on walls and delivering union leaflets. He had to interrupt his studies and went back to Cyprus for two years. He worked in bars during that time to earn money to go back to school and graduate.

When they moved back to Cyprus, they joined a left-wing party, probably the only opposition party in North Cyprus at that time. They left the party, CTP, in early 90s. I think in the early 2000s, it turned out to be worse than a rightwing party, a fascist party. Before that time, being a member of a left-wing party actually meant something in Cyprus. It meant you supported a united Cyprus. It meant you were strongly against fascism and separation. The president of North Cyprus was Rauf Denktaş for many years until 2005. There were a few people in Cyprus who openly talked about how he triggered and encouraged the idea of a divided Cyprus, and about the people who got murdered because of this. The left-wing party that I'm talking about was the most prominent opponent of his administration. In the presidential elections of 2005, the candidate of the party became the first so-called leftist president of North Cyprus, who promised to work for a united Cyprus. I say "so-called" because the party took a more hypocritical stance later, and there was less transparency.

People who believe in resisting this division, and who wish for a united Cyprus are becoming smaller in number. In summer 2017, I was sitting under a bougainvillea tree in Strovolos. I was there because a man named Kiriakos had passed away; he was our friend and an active supporter of peace in Cyprus. I remember I was sitting on a veranda next to a friend at his house, in a very Cypriot neighborhood. As cigarette smoke thickened, he said, "One day, they will say that there used to be some people called Cypriots, who have become extinct, like dinosaurs." I burst into tears, for everything was unbearable. The mind and the island share the same imprisonment. I was in tears and he said it was a good thing, for he couldn't even cry.'

I attended a college that was near our house in Kyrenia. I used to walk home from school most of the time. At that time, the college was supposed to be one of the bests in North Cyprus for students who were eager to study abroad at a university. Our first history lesson was about Cyprus and what had happened between 1963 and 1974. Our teacher played a video that showed the results of the political conflict of that period. There were stills of dead people in bathtubs, bloodshed on the streets, people killing each other, and then proud, heroic soldiers. It was a dreadful video and I was only like ten years old. You don't teach history like that! I went home that day and I told mum what I was made to watch. That teacher was a Turkish nationalist and a fascist. Years later mum told me that she should've called the college and told them that it was the last thing a child must see. It was brainwashing and every single of his lessons stank of fascist propaganda. This is how they teach history in Cyprus, every Cypriot child learns history in a similar way.'

Thus the magic began to diminish in its own way. Instead of gushing, it fell in drops from the beaker of childhood, the innocence of believing in good and evil, in human and monster, in the creatures that were anything but human.

And then, it disappeared. Lost like Nilüfer, in the strange place she had once called home, the foreign within the city of her birth.

'I grew up in Kyrenia. It is a beautiful city, but it used to be nicer and safer back in the 90s, I think. I am not really fond of it anymore because you barely see any Cypriots around nowadays. I never had any xenophobic feelings against another culture, and I don't now either, but the Turkish migrants, who moved to Cyprus have changed our cities, our traditions. Their government by encouraging more people to move to Cyprus, much more than this piece of land can carry, triggers a Turkish culture being assimilated into Cypriot culture. Ironically though, it is Turkish-Cypriots and our Cypriot environment that are becoming more

Turkish and less Cypriot. I know that for some cases Cyprus is an escape for the Turks who move here. It's more liberal and secular. They can never have a Cypriot liberal life in Turkey. It is a secular country where you can openly express your religious and political beliefs. They say North Cyprus is the filthy garden of Turkey, like its backyard filled with rubbish. The Turkish government sends its criminals here, and our government knows about all this. They own casinos and brothels, any sort of criminal activity that you can think of. I mentioned I used to walk to college. Now I can't imagine myself strolling around Kyrenia without being harassed, without being gazed at, without being insulted, late at night, especially if you're in the "wrong" place. Who knows, you might even get raped. We read about these incidents on the news nowadays. It is a corrupted and a crowded culture now.'

Even the magic of friendship could not keep the spell of love oriented towards the land of her birth.

'I am very fortunate to have a Greek-Cypriot family (in my life). When they opened the borders in 2003, we crossed the checkpoint in Nicosia with my parents, and that was the time when I first met my Greek-Cypriot family. My parents formed a very close friendship with them and they became our closest family friends. We have had countless summer holidays together, travelled, had delicious Cypriot food, and long conversations about ourselves, about our island. When they met my grandfather, Maria, the mother of that family, was in utter shock. She always saw pictures of my grandfather but had never met him in person. When they met that first time, she felt very emotional and shaken, for apparently my granddad looked exactly like her father. What is funnier is that Stephanos, her husband, looked just like my father. The same bridged nose, arched thick eyebrows. They wore the same vest jacket and shared the same political

views. They were very close friends. My father was a doctor but he never cared a lot about his daily attire, to be honest. In the summer, he used to go to the hospital wearing shorts and one of his Cuban shirts, with leaves and flower prints, so colourful. I've never seen another doctor like him. He loved summer and he was very outgoing and social. Stephanos is quite the same; his appearance is the last thing on his mind. They valued what's within. Whenever they got together, they used to open up beers and set the barbeque and smoke a few cigarettes over their endless conversations. My father got very ill in April 2016. He was in the last stages of cancer and Maria and Stephanos were with me at the hospital everyday. I am very fortunate to have them in my life. My father is no longer with us, but I'm happy that we still get together to cook food and drink beer…we still continue to have our traditional summer nights.'

But Nilüfer began to hate the island, its memories pained her, and its present pushed her aside. There is nothing here, she would tell herself. What future do I have here? She ran away, searching for that thing in the streets of London, in the books lying on her desk that talked identity, post-colonialism and conflict, in the essays she wrote pondering over questions that touched corners of her being. It was during one of her returns that she had met Aurora. The Aurora who had been dazzled by the island, whose energy was bursting with passion for its hidden secrets, for its healing and for those laying their hands to heal it of its scars.

'Before I met her, it was more like hatred and I despised everything about Cyprus, about its people, about its past, about what it could offer. She, Aurora, showed me the beauty of the island. She changed my perception. She is Cyprus, so colourful, so much energy. As I began to love her, I began to love Cyprus. I even grew fonder of my hometown. Perhaps a few years ago I

didn't even like being a Cypriot, I didn't like my home. I always had this anger against it. I am sort of calmer now. I show more tolerance to the things that happened in Cyprus and maybe to people as well. I think what Cyprus means to me is still a thing to happen; I think it is still a journey of my becoming. I think Cyprus and I are both on a journey and we will figure it out. It's like magic.'

Aurora's magic.

Borders

I am BENITO

We should be proud
of who we are and our past history!

COURAGE

You read Cyprus, you read 1974 and the first thought that pops out is invasion. Or maybe nothing pops out because you have not watched the parades year after year along the streets of Nicosia, Limassol, Larnaca, Pafos in celebration of independence, watched black and white clips of who shooting whom or shooting back who by whom during school assemblies, heard EOKA, Makarios and maybe even Nikos Sampson passed round like bread at the dinner table, at the taverna along Makenzie, at the bus stop, falling words with the crumbles and spit. But just know, or pretend to understand, that the equation Cyprus + 1974 = invasion. Then even if I add in Turkey, and coup and civil war, Greek Cypriots and Turkish Cypriots, South and North, and then numbers, many many of them, you will not run off, bewildered, and we can calmly zoom out, and start talking Western politics with Henry Kissinger, James Callaghan and on and on. And we could go on and on. And on. But let us return to 1974.

Famagusta. Chaos. Bombs. Crying. Children wrapped in whatever blanket, cloth, rag could be grabbed on the way out of the house as mother, father, brother, sister flee. Clutching little heads to knocking hearts. Trembles, trembling. Neighbor shadowing neighbor. Before the thud of the army troop. With their flags. Rifles. Their fury. Neighbours pile into cars.

Maybe enough time to check documents. Papers in their hands. But don't dare look back. Maybe Lot's wives are in this crowd. But cars furiously accelerate. Forward. With open/closed eyes. Away. To the side. From the "other"'side. Greek-Cypriot South. Turkish-Cypriot North. Call it chaos.

But it was measurable. There was a direction, like a whirlwind moving with the wind. A barometer checking its reading. A compass in hand.

Not all the cars fleeing the territory of Famagusta were Greek-Cypriot. Families of British dependents and army reserves had also been caught up in these beginning stages of the civil war. However, there was a calm in the humdrum of their vehicles as they headed to the British bases, the only parts of the island they knew would be removed from the upcoming slaughter. One such car was on its way down, blowing up even more dust into the already foul air. The family was quiet against the sounds of the engine. Rocks were flying. Outside. But as they came onto less dusty roads and the air cleared, another car appeared behind them. Or maybe it had been there the whole time. Since Famagusta. It followed them, upon their tail. A little too close for comfort. From the blurred reflection in the rearview mirror, the British officer could make out a young man at the wheel and a woman at the back holding a small child. His heart may have slowed for the couple did not appear threatening, he may even have relaxed his clenched jaw. Right, need to sort this out, he may have thought and then indicated that he was pulling over and that the car behind should do the same.

Benito parked his car behind the British vehicle. He watched the officer briskly make his way towards him. It was hard to understand the expression on the British officer's face behind the dark shades. Maybe a slight stiffness in the lips. Benito lowered the window and the man was soon there, not too keen on friendliness or patience in the midst of war. Who was he? What was he doing following a British convoy? Benito apologised, and in his low voice explained as much as he could (or was willing at that point, as much as being in a not so peaceful time allowed him) how he, an Italian, was afraid for his family, and was fleeing Famagusta for…for…for protection. He knew the officer was headed towards the Dhekelia base, which was assumed immune from the war. That is all he was looking for right then: safety. Please, could he and his family follow behind the officer?

'You are not British, you cannot follow us so closely,' the officer barked in reply.

'But we have Turkish plates. They (the Greek army) will see us and shoot us,' Benito pleaded.

The officer shrugged and walked back to his own car. But even after the warning, and the repeated glares from the officer's rearview mirror, Benito followed the British plates. He was tense throughout the whole journey, his eyes narrowed, fixed upon the car ahead. But there were no more stops nor second warnings. Even when the car ahead turned into the British base, and Benito drove on west, he remained just as tense and focused, just as quiet as the long journey through the night. If we can just reach it, he thought, if we can just reach Limassol, all will be well.

'My parents were born in Larnaca but our ancestors are Italian. My father's family came to Cyprus in 1722. My mother's family, they originate from Slovenia. But my mother knew nothing about it but the name. On my mother's side they are half-Italian, half-Slovenian.'

Benito's grandparents, similarly to other Italians who emigrated to Cyprus during that period, were businessmen. In 1865, Antonio Lorenzo Mantovani, or Grandfather Mantovani, established a family-run shipping agency in Larnaca,

A.L. Mantovani & Sons Ltd. The company was successful, and soon expanded into tourism, allowing travelers onto their represented passenger liners heading either to Australia or Italy. When the time came, this heritage was passed on to Father Mantovani, Uncle Mantovani, Cousins Mantovani and Benito Mantovani. What was passed on, generation to generation, was more than an established business, but a culture, and a direct connection to their ancestors' land and language. For Benito, this would become something he would hold very dear: the histories of the Mantovanis.

This, of course, was not always the case for young Benito. Especially growing up in a small Cypriot town, attending a local Cypriot school and interacting with the Cypriot children next door. Greek became the tongue of choice and the language that most appealed to his present. Though there was a decent community of Italians at the time, approximately 1200 of either first, second or third generation immigrants, Benito struggled to acquire his mother's native tongue, Italian.

'I was talking Italian with the family at home but not very good. Italian was the "official" language of the Mantovanis, our ancestry. My parents would say you can't write, you're not able to talk. My mother had cousins in Trieste on her father's side and, therefore, sent me as a student from the ages of sixteen to eighteen. I spent the summers there to learn Italian.'

The summers passed slowly in Trieste. So too the sounds of the Romance language that flowed between Benito and his relatives in Trieste, and then back again, there and back again. Soon, Benito found himself forgetting his Greek, as he left the island to attend boarding school in Somerset, a Business and Administration degree at the Univeristy of Indiana, and an Italian Literature degree in Trieste University,

Italy. In total, Benito was away from Cyprus for over five years. But after each passing year, his heart still ached for the small town of Larnaca. And not just his.

'Generally, the students coming from Cyprus who stay away from Cyprus for long, stay abroad. I was the exception. If you stay away too long and get accustomed to the life there and you don't have a link or a family waiting for you, you may not come back because you get used to the new life. I had family here, I had part of the business to take over. I knew it was a matter of time before I came back.'

BE COURAGEOUS

'In 1939, the Second World War was declared. My father and his brothers, who were described as Italians by the British, became refugees. They were taken to Kyrenia castle as prisoners of war. My family transferred from Kyrenia to Prodromos because the Italian internees were transferred by the British to the Berengaria Hotel. This venue had closed to the public in winter and it offered better facilities than Kyrenia Castle (as a detainment facility). Then in the winter they transferred them to the Le Merida Hotel. So, my mother, my grandmother and I moved to Troodos and then we hear, without us knowing, that they put them in military trucks and took them to Famagusta Port. We rushed there but we couldn't see anything. They had put them on a ship and taken them to Uganda. Only years later, in 1945, did they put them on a ship and bring them back to Cyprus. I still remember the censored letter with black lines over what the censors thought their prisoners shouldn't read or write. So on that day in 1945, we hear they are in Famagusta Port, and I went with my mother and brother as quickly as we could there to bring them back home.'

BE ENCOURAGED

In 1960, the Republic of Cyprus declared the official recognition of two ethnic communities, the Greek and the Turkish Cypriot. Under the umbrella of the two ethnic communities, three religious groups were also constitutionally recognised, mainly the Latin Catholics, the Armenians and the Maronites as branches of the Greek Cypriot community. With the uprising of EOKA extremists and Greek nationalism across the island, the religious communities maintained a low profile, a tactic of survival and peacekeeping. Benito returned to Cyprus in 1961 to take his place at the Mantovani offices in Larnaca and at the headquarters in Famagusta, the main port at the time. He became a witness to the fear of speaking out by the religious minority communities, being both part of the Latin Catholic community and having married an Armenian wife.

'Nobody took any action to silence the minorities. Some of the members of minority groups were afraid to express themselves because they felt -and wrongly did so-that, after a bitter conflict, minorities could be suppressed. This proved wrong because nobody bothered the minorities and any member working in the Government continued to work and get promotions. My response was, why should the Catholics keep a low profile? I had to build up the community's ego, to make them understand that they have rights according to the Constitution. They are a recognised religious group, so why should they remain invisible? I started writing letters, one every two months, telling the Church what I did, who I met, which Minister etc., what I had organised, what we did, and I repeated that we are a constitutionally recognised community, irrespective of our size, and we have rights. We should be proud of who we are and our past history!'

The island's landscape played an important role in accentuating the history of the Latin community. Just look around, Benito said, the Venetian Walls around the Old City of Nicosia, the structure of Kolossi Castle, the port of Famagusta, declared during the Venetian period as the centre of the Mediterranean, the Order of Saint Joseph of the Apparition, the first hospital and pharmacy in 1844. Each a reminder, each a powerful memory of belonging, then and now, a footprint not yet washed away by the tide. Be proud, Benito repeated, be proud and don't forget who you are.

Gradually, pride became an active component within the Latin Catholic community. There is something irresistible about Benito, his charisma, the power of his energy. It was no fluke that he was not only granted but maintained a seat as a Member of Parliament, representative of the Latin Catholic Community, for twenty-five years.

As he drives along the streets of Limassol, there are memories that spring to him, memories of times when it had not always been easy, when he too wished to remain quiet, under a cover because there was no one else to protect him. Just he and a thin piece of fabric clutched in his hands. But with each memory comes a thought, and that thought with the changing of traffic lights from red, yellow to green. The speed of moving forward, of taking that road rather than the other, of heading home. Courage, dear heart, courage.

I am YANN

You have to respect the flag and everything. For me it is an obligation.

There are photos sitting on every shelf of the living room. Older black and white shots of his grandfather, grandmother, his mother and aunt still in Congo, framed portraits of his sons in Cypriot army uniform, his daughter cradling a baby, smiling at the lens. It is a museum of memories, visual reminders of blood's strength against water. There on paper his family occupies two continents, Africa and Europe. Now, as he speaks, he thinks of his children who have taken to movement and exploration, living in Cyprus, France and Canada. They are far, and at times he mourns over the fact that it is only technology that connects them now, that only through a screen can he enter their lives. But in that room, his family gather, their faces watching their father as he breathes air into their persons, through stories of how they came to be.

As he talks, I can see another photo, not present on the counter although it could very well have been. The setting is a long room, a corridor dim despite the intent of the naked bulbs, arranged above the heads of persons scurrying here and there under the eye of its glow. The floor mopped that morning and I imagine the whiff of bleach still lingering over tiles that are already smudged with fresh blood and mud. In the corner, a man lies on a makeshift stretcher, a grown man, dark hair covering part of his face, and a coarse beard covering his jaw. He is broad in shoulder, he is broad all around. There is nothing inherently special about him.

He clutches his side, a man in his forty brought to tears over the bloody mess he has made on his skin, what is left of his shirt and the floor beneath him. There are women gathered around him, let's count four, their dresses of discolored material, bent over him, holding down his arms, his legs, another staring into the camera, about to command the scene into action. The women's hair is dark, their eyes are dark, and one nurse's skin is dark, darker than the rest of the team, her lips fuller, her gaze fixed on the man's wound. She blends in but at the same time catches your eye as you glance over the black and white still. In the midst of the 1974 invasion hitting Cyprus, in a scene featuring a hospital clinic, the small Congolese nurse was a rarity, especially as only a handful of black peoples resided across the island. Yet there she was, loyal, determined, her heart feeling for the soldiers, for her father's homeland, for her brothers and sisters dying all around her. She was there. Like a photo, she is caught in that memory, the diminishing colors and the fading faces, but the blood, life and death, they are frozen, still.

The war ended, the Green Line was marked out, dividing the island, North and South. The main post office that after the division was caught on the 'wrong' side. The nurse in her uniform could no longer spend a few minutes cycling down to the post office once a week. It pained her the changes occurring every day, even upon her daily habits. Every time she walked outside, ready for another day at the busy practice, she could not help but glance back across her shoulder to the Kyrenia mountains, brandishing the Turkish flag, reminding her of a past life. Even today, retired from her practice, and with the borders open, she refuses to support, refuses to accept the changes.

'She saw. She saw the injuries. She was treating the Greek Cypriots. She saw a lot of things. Worse, she cannot freely go to

light a candle or to gather at the grave of her father who had died in 1971, and buried in the north of Nicosia under occupation since 1974. That's why. That's why.'

Yann was three months old when he had first arrived on the island. His mother held him to her chest as she surveyed the Larnaca Port, the fishermen, the hubbub of the sailors, the old men playing tavli at a bench not far off. Yann's grandfather had not seen his home for over thirty-five years. Nor had his relatives seen him since his departure to find a life in Africa.

'But as my grandfather left Cyprus for a long time and didn't send back news during the last twenty years, here in Cyprus the relatives say, "Maybe this guy die in Africa".'

Yann's grandfather was eager to point out the changes he was witnessing that had occurred between his departure in the 1920s, when he was around twenty-eight years old, and his arrival in 1955, whilst his family clutched their belongings and followed him to the bus stop. They were all exhausted from the weeks travelling but for this last bus ride they pulled out their last leg of will, if not energy. They had no choice.

'It was a big trip, a long trip. A long long trip. We took a train from the city we lived in until Albertville city. There we took a small ship from Tanganyika Lake to Kigoma port in the Republic of Tanzania. We changed again, we took the train until we crosssed all the country to the maritime port of Dar - es - Salam; and from there, we took the big boat in the Indian Ocean to the Red Sea and when we arrived at Port Said, we changed again and the boat, a small one until Larnaca port.'

At this period of his life, Yann's grandfather had only one dream: to spend his last days in the land of his birth, Cyprus, and be buried there. On the 26th of October 1955, the same year when the Greek Cypriot insurrectional EOKA movement against British rule revolted, that dream finally took its first steps on land.

They caught the last bus to Nicosia. The following day, from Nicosia, the following day, grandfather, his two daughters and grandson, boarded an early bus headed to Troodos that not only acted as transport for people but also as the distributor of mail for the Soleia Valley. After explaining to the bus driver where the family was headed and working out which bus stop would be closest to the village of a niece he hoped would take his small family in, the grandfather settled back into his seat to watch the world outside. The fields of wheat, the goats being herded back to their enclosures, now and again cars streaming past at a maximum of 70kmh. He may have been thinking about his wife back in Congo, what could she be doing then? What about his friends, were they thinking of him as he did of them? The congregation he had left, was there a Catholic Church to attend here? Maybe it would be simpler to attend the Orthodox Church run by his niece's husband, the pope of the village. They would be staying with them for a while. At one point he raised his forehead from the cool glass window and looked back at his grandson, little Yann, who, exhausted from the journey, was finally asleep. The baby had been a surprise, a shock really, especially to the planning of this trip. His seventeen-year-old daughter's pregnancy had been kept a secret by the women from him, the patriarch of the family. *Romeo and Juliet,* Yann's grandfather may have muttered, rolling his eyes to the heavens as if challenging them to contradict him. But, at least, they were here.

'You know, in this period, Congo was a Belgian colony. My mum didn't have plan to move to Cyprus. She was born in Congo

and was very integrated in Congo. When she met my father, who was working in a mining company as an executive, they had a secret love story. It was kept secret with the complicity of my grandmother who never agreed to the project moving to Cyprus. Mix couple in this colonial era were rare almost non-existent. It was more than normal to see a European to have a love story with an African lady but not vice versa. Also, during that era there was a small problem of discrimination...My grandmother never disclosed the information on who impregnated my mother to my grandfather. Finally, when I was born my grandfather understood that the father is not European, of course he is African. But who exactly? It was a secret between my mother and my grandmother. My mother had me while she was still a minor and according to the law of the colony, my grandfather had the right to exercise authority over my mother. Therefore, he forced her to follow him to Cyprus! But my grandmother stayed behind.'

It had not been a simple task to convince his daughter to leave her life in Congo, despite his promises of a better life. In all honesty, he needed his daughter more than she needed a new life in Cyprus. She was a qualified nurse, and he could trust her with his life or whatever was left of it, and right then he feared there was very little left. The sudden decision to leave Congo back to his birthplace was a whim of a decision, in fulfillment of a strong desire, and almost dread of being buried beside strangers instead of the village cemetery in his country of birth, beside his mother and father. Yann's grandfather sighed deeply, he could feel a headache coming. The aching of his bones, the tension within his stomach area. All he wanted at that point was a clean bed on which to lay his head , and hoped his cousin would not be too surprised at this unexpected visit and favour. Back in the day, his niece had been known among the family members for her benevolent hospitality. He hoped thirty-five years had not changed that. She will welcome me, he convinced himself. All I need now is rest. Rest, rest. We will visit my village in a few days, after we rest, Yann's grandfather decided.

'Oh, it was not easy. It was not easy because when we went two days after to see the village of my grandfather, it was a shock for my mum. My mother told my grandfather, "If you bring me from Africa, move to Cyprus to stay in this village, I prefer to go back to my country." At the time, the village, if you compare with the town in Congo where we usually live, there is a big difference. There was no electricity in this village, for example. It was very cold for her accustomed to the hot and humid tropical climate. The village seemed too small and less attractive. There was almost no black people here in Cyprus. According to what my mother told me, there were only one or two mixed families. There was also a lot of gossip. People thought that all those who were returning after a long stay of expatriation in Africa came back with big fortunes in their suitcases. Our modest family has not escaped this kind of prejudice.'

When Yann was old enough, his mother found work as an assistant nurse in a private clinic in Nicosia to support her family. She left the village to live closer to her workplace. She would spend the rest of her life working and living in the capital, growing to understand and love this part of herself, her Cypriot blood. Her son grew up surrounded by his Greek Cypriot relatives, a child whose first 'glossa', language, was Greek. However, being the only child with dark skin in the Dimotiko, primary, school, did not stop him from making friends or topping his class, becoming the '*Alpha Alpha*' high achieving student of his class.

However, after his first year at Dimotiko, Yann's father, who had kept regular contact by letters, asked and obtained the consent of Yann's mother and grandfather for his son to return to visit him in Congo. This holiday would last for over thirty years for little Yann. Soon the little was waving goodbye to his mother, whose presence for the next three decades would be limited to letters and a rare visit. Through her writing and then phone calls (up to 1990, international direct phone calls with Congo were nonexistent), her stories of life in Cyprus would keep her son connected to that side of his ancestry, nourishing his dreams to return, at the very least, for a visit.

'I stayed separate from my mother for a long time and when I finally came back here it was in 1997. I left my family in Congo, my wife and four children. The fifth one was born after, my wife was pregnant when I left. There was a lot of trouble during this period. I lost my job in the mining company. I lost everything so when I arrive in Cyprus, I had no choice. There was an urgent need for money. How to find money? You have to work. Any job I was candidate.'

Despite having been an executive in a public mining company back in Congo, the only job he could find, at least in the beginning, was as a labourer in a manufacturing company based in Nicosia. It was not an easy job nor did the working conditions alleviate any hardships. Foreign labour was not an uncommon sight in the streets of the capital; the 1990s had seen a surge of workers arriving on the island to fill in the gaps left agape in the low-skilled market, a factor that was responsible for stalling the growth of the economy. Reacting to pressure from multiple employers across the state, the government had relaxed its borders in welcome to what they described as a 'temporary phenomenon'. Expendable and ephemeral, and let's keep it that way, they thought and shook hands on it. The problem with passing legislation is that it diffuses into the attitude of the public, constructing reservations and perceptions, institutionalising and normalising: if the legal state defines temporary as temporary, then temporary you will be in the eyes of its population. A foreigner, an outsider. Someone to leave, someone to go. To throw out when the country is finished with you.

'I will tell you an anecdote. When I was working in the factory only the supervisor who was an engineer knew my profile, knew who I was. There was one young boy too. So after four months, I was going to leave my job because I told my comrade that I found a job at the school and I will teach there. During lunch my friend told to another Cypriot worker that Yann will leave the factory .

"Why? Not good salary? He go back to his country?"

"No, he will be a teacher."

"A teacher? You teach in Cyprus? You!?"

He thought it was a joke. Why was it a surprise to him that I will teach in Cyprus? I would be teaching in a European private school.

"Ah kalo, kalo," he said when I told him.

You see?

In 1997, when I signed the contract at the school, I had to change my status at the Department of Migration from labour worker to teacher. I went to fill in the form. Then they sent me the response. I have the letter until now: "We have received your application. You have not the right to be employed in Cyprus like a teacher so we ask you to leave Cyprus by 15 days.' Guys (from the Immigration Office) *bring me this letter. My mum was working at this time. It was in the evening.*

"You are Mr Yann?"

"Yes, I am Mr Yann."

"We bring you a letter and you have to sign the receipt there."

It was in English. I ask this guy, "You are young. I suppose your mother is alive?"

"My mother is alive."

"Ok, you see the house here. Is my mum's house. I am the only son of my mum. The only, we are now two. Do you think she has

not the right to have this family together? Why you ask me to leave?"'

At their next opportunity, mother and son marched to the Immigration Office. Yann's mother was livid. When it came to their turn to speak to the officer on rota, the room, with its damp and thin walls, could not contain her. She was not big in size but at that moment her presence outweighed any other, behind or in front of the office.

"'*You asked my family,*"' she began, her eyes glaring into the officer's attempts to avoid her stare, "'*my son to go back (to Congo) because he is poor. Why not I have the right like everyone else to live with my son and my grandchildren*"

My mother was furious and did not understand this discrimination. Why don't children born to Cypriot women not automatically acquire Cypriot nationality? Or why do they not even have the right to remain with their mother and find a job that matched their education and profile?!'

The meeting was long enough to make her intentions clear if her request was not granted, who she would contact, what would be their response, and, most importantly, what would be the consequences for the Immigration Office, no, not only, but the government of the state once all this discriminatory practice came to light. It would be on this officer's neck, and the blame would be all on him, that was obvious, and spelled out perfectly clear.

'Two days after, the officer invited us to the Number One of the Immigration. After we leave the office, the Number One says, "Ask that guy to change this letter. The Number One says this guy must stay in Cyprus." They brought me a new letter affording me the right to work and stay here.'

Following the amendment voted in the Cypriot Parliament in 1999, children born of Cypriot women automatically acquired Cypriot citizenship. Finally, after a few more adventures at the Immigration Office, Yann managed to obtain Cypriot citizenship, not only for himself but also for his five children when they arrived on the island. And one by one, the part-Cypriots became recognized as full citizens.

Yann's son is in the room, as his father points to a photo. A man in his twenties, tall with soft warm eyes. It is the same face as the one sitting in the neighbouring chair, though slightly younger in his military uniform. There is a smile, proud, though his father's pride overpowers the son's, maybe because his smile expands and contracts, his hands move this way and that, with precision, with care, and then his voice fills like a cup and slowly allows words to flow. They become everything, they become a truth for everybody else. Fantastic will be fantastic, and disasters will be disasters. He sits looking at his son, content, as if the destination he had been walking towards all these years has finally been reached. They are here, now.

'Holding this passport for us is not just a pleasure. You have to respect the flag and everything. For me it is an obligation.'

I smile at the son's determined words. At first it appears like mimicry under the gaze of his father, but blood is strong, blood is loyal, their blood writes them to an order.

After a pause, the father nods, a slow heavy nod.

'I am Cypriot. Cyprus is my second 'Patrida' because I have a lot of story in Cyprus. Yes, I feel it.'

I am MARCEL

I don't like borders or boundaries.
I like cultures and how they are different.

'A border is what they draw on maps. But maps are not reality. Reality is reality. So, you can actually walk from one place to another, this is reality. But what is made is you're gonna get caught by the police if you don't have this special book, this passport. It would be nice if people were allowed to do these things, do as they like. But someone else invented this thing that we are not allowed to move around and we are just fighting to lift this structure away.'

December 2011. Kykkos Street, Nicosia. It is cool. The huddled group raise their hoods against the breeze. Some are painting letters. Their brushes are stiff in their fingers as hands move up and down in long black strokes. 'B'. The strokes form a big, bold, blatant 'B'. Possibly spelling 'Buffer' or 'Borders' or even 'Bullshit'. Maybe just 'BS'. A few hooded figures are gathered around a cooking pot, helping themselves to a stew: an assortment of beans, vegetables and potatoes. *Hearty*. A couple make their way towards a tent, embracing, stepping delicately over the litter from last night's celebrations. They do not mind the eyes of the guards glaring at them from either side, right and left, north and south, disgusted, cursing. *It is all about love*, some will say, as if love, whatever it is or was, can be the answer to any problem, to the problem they have at hand. But for now they are creating their own solutions, together. There will be a speech later by an older youth in a tie and jacket, spitting out words such as 'enosi', union, between his memorized

English sentences, followed by an open debate with another young man, who is determined to fight 'enosi' with 'diairesi', division. It will be a long night of talking. More food will be brought followed by some singing, some guitar strumming, some intuitive dancing and then the slow crawling back into pitched tents, just before dawn or maybe just after. This is how Cyprus's division is being resolved. Politics sleeping on the streets of 'No Man's Land'.

'The answer, my friend, is blowin' in the wind/The answer is blowin' in the wind.' [1]

In light of the escalating tensions between Greek and Turkish Cypriots, Major General Peter Young, a commander of the British forces stationed in Cyprus at that time, drew a line across Cyprus with a green pencil, separating northern and southern regionsin 1963. Respectively, appointing 'Turkish' and 'Greek' domains. After the invasion of 1974, the 'Green Line' was extended to 300km (across the whole island) and was declared impassable unless under extreme (official) circumstances. The UN stationed their own patrol to guard the border, and continue to police the region to this day. It was only in April 2003, after a 30-year ban, that the crossing restrictions were eased and movement between each side was permitted through passport-controlled crossing points. The twenty-four hour crossing point at Ledra is one of the busiest and is used by both locals and tourists daily.

'It was a crazy place because we were in this one road protected by political grey areas where there was two armies from both sides with a third army in the middle. But really it sounds much more rough than it was. For us it was camping and we were hanging with people, chilling, cooking food there, making tents and so on.'

---

1 *Bob Dylan, 'Blowin' in the Wind.' (Warner Bros Inc.: 1962)*

The Occupy Buffer Zone protest (OBZ) began in October 2011 with the aim to 'occupy' the already 'occupied' area between the two crossing points on Ledra, the zone controlled by UN officials. Protesters came together from all walks of life to connect in their frustration over the current political situation of the country. Specifically, the waiting game that had ensued ever since Cyprus entered the European Union and the annual promises that politicians and presidents were quick to make but even quicker to backtrack over whether or not the division between the North and South will be lifted. However, not all those participating in OBZ aspired after a unified island.

'Everyone of us there at OBZ had their own ideas about what they wanted. Politically. They might have not agreed on everything and different ideas of what could have been ideal but they all agreed what they have now is completely ridiculous. If we unite the two countries maybe one guy would say, "... oh everything will be great." The other guy would say, "...yeah it would be ok but I'd rather it was split." Or something like that. Everyone agreed it's ridiculous as it was now and that one or the other would be better. Everyone was much more chilled about the solution.'

There is a smell, a blend of leftover chili, fresh dog waste, body sweat and mosquito repellant. The whole group had their own scent of familiarity. Something the dogs could recognise as friend not foe. Even when faces changed. It was like they were all one. Within this small community of protesters, there were skins and tongues of accents that stood out from the rest. The 'border' sometimes became a 'borter' or boghter', a beautiful thing that sound, that mixing of palettes and colors, jazz in its humility. Multiculturalism, somebody may have used, a multicultural congregation.

'As a traveler, I barely knew about the conflict and division. I

just thought, OK there are two different people, Greek and Turkish. I wasn't into politics so I didn't make a big deal of it when I came to North Cyprus. Within one to two hours I was crossing Ledra Street and there were protesters who were like, "Hey dude, come on and stay." So, I stayed there for some time.

Now, I was born in the Czech Republic. Living in a small town, going to school. I came from a weird family because my brother has a mental illness so everything was a bit hectic in places. I was always into mathematics, sciences and music so I started studying programming computers. I was programming first steps when I was like twelve and when I was fifteen/sixteen I was making websites. I picked it up without school or anything. I dropped out of school and I was doing some basic jobs like security around the Czech Republic. But the Czech Republic has problems. You know it's like really famous with beer. The largest consumption of beer per capita by far like 40% more than Germany, which is second. This is a crazy amount of beer! People just like alcohol. When I was living there I couldn't say what was it like living there because I didn't have any comparison but now I can say it's like people are kind of scared and, you know, not very active, not very loud, you know, on their own and they get drunk and only then can they let loose. With Communism, a lot of people were not allowed to say what they thought for a long time, and now they're still affected to say what they think. There's this kind of polarity. It's actually a good country, I'm not like trying to make it sound horrible, no, it's developed like now last year it's very close to Germany with developments so it's fine but it has this alcohol/drug problem.

So, one day, I just got pissed off with everything. I got a job at one factory. It was just a boring job, and I was saving money for a year. After a year I went off. I started hitchhiking through Europe. I had a tent, clothes, backpack, little cooker, little pot and paper maps. I walked everywhere by foot or I hitchhiked, maybe bus. First, I went Greece. I went around and all the way down to Kalamata. My plan was to go to Africa, it was the carrot for me. But planning for this I had to get vaccinations for some things and then someone told me that it is not one vaccination, actually, you need to get multiple. So, one vaccine and then a few months later another one so I left Czech Republic and it took me a few weeks to get to Greece then I turned around. Through Slovenia, Croatia, Albania, Amsterdam to France.

I was not scared…maybe a few times. Once I was scared was a few days after I started. Some group of guys who had some bottles of wine drinking from a bag. I started talking to them. They said they knew a place I could crash. I didn't know how to get out of the town. It was a village area, small town. One of the guys said he will find me a place to stay and in the end he didn't. He did some cocaine and was up all night. He started talking to me so long and I was like, "Come on, I need to sleep!" It was a bit weird because I didn't expect that. That was a minor thing. Other time was when I woke up in the night next to Budapest in a tent. There was a wild boar sniffing on the sides of my tent. I was really scared but when I woke up nothing happened. I just didn't move. I was in a sleeping bag, so he wasn't doing anything. He was just sniffing for like a minute. He was like big. But later he left, and that was finished.

Then I think I was going north to Sweden to find some job. I needed money for food and everything. Didn't find a job there but someone told me to go to Holland. I crossed to Holland. I hitchhiked there a little bit. It's a **very very** *small island. I was moving around and asking people randomly for jobs.*

Met a guy who said he can't pay much but there's a fence that needs fixing. I was like, "Yeah, its OK in exchange for food and a place to stay." I started fixing his fence and he said, "You're pretty good at this, let's start building a house." There was this black wooden cottage. He wanted to break it down because it was old and build a new one but he didn't want to get new permission for that. So, he decided to actually take everything from inside and build new cottage inside the old one. Basically we built a house inside a house.

But soon it was October and I could feel getting cold. I needed to go south with my tent. I hitchhiked to Serbia, then Turkey. I spent two months doing random things, moving around, lost my passport, found my passport, found some people, stayed in a hotel. People in Turkey are really really nice to travelers so I was really enjoying it there but there was a problem. I couldn't get a job without a work permit and for that I have to have a visa. This for any company who would offer me good job, good money. You know, like jobs in an office not cleaning potatoes. But they say like you have to stay here for fifteen years because they have a lot of trouble setting things up legally. I said, "No." And I moved on and went to Cyprus. December 2011.

I came just before Christmas and stayed in Ledra. Except for February and March for a few weeks as I was in Limassol doing some construction and then I came back. It was just before a lot of police running to the place and they beat all the protesters up. When I came back I was really sad about this for missing it. I wanted to support my new friends.'

On the 1st of January, in an effort to escape the cold, the protesters migrated to the abandoned buildings located within the buffer zone. These buildings later became the headquarters of the movement, where general assemblies were being hosted for the current community and potential new members. On the 14th of January, the UNFICYP demanded for the protesters to evacuate the buffer zone, claiming the activities did not follow UN-approved regulations. The protesters refused. Though the UN did not proceed with a follow-up removal through force, the Republic of Cyprus revealed its own impatience in a violent police raid on the 6th of April 2012. A police force, armed with helmets, batons and guns, broke into the buildings occupied by the protesters and let loose a tirade of assault against the men and women living inside. Beatings, sexual assault and a mass of arrests followed against unarmed youths and OBZ was swiftly and viciously dismantled in the matter of one night. At the aftermath of the attack, the movement slowly faded and by June 2012, it was once again a mere dream, a slogan on a cardboard cut-out, a story of trying to belong, to connect, to be.

'I left earlier. I had to leave because I didn't have anything. No money to live on. One friend of mine I met at OBZ said he had a friend near Paphos. She said we could stay there some time and help make some money so I came there. We kinda settled. Me, my friend and the woman I was staying with. They are older people, British. I was staying there, chilling for about a year. Working on computers, trying programming again. We had some idea for some businesses but it didn't work. So, I was taking care of the garden, fooling around with the cats. It was nice. Learnt a lot of English there. It was a very different idea of Cyprus because the area around Paphos is all English people. British retired community. It was chilled. Every now and then there was a concert that was made by a friend of a friend. After all the stress of travelling, it was nice to slow and settle down.

After a year I left for Nicosia. That was the end of Paphos. I had very little money at the time so I stayed in an apartment. Shared living. Really horrible place. The owner first seemed nice in the end turned out to be a complete freak. There were some very sketchy people there. There was someone who stole my laptop. The other one borrowed fifty euros from me. Then he left and in the end there was one woman who was living with me she didn't pay the rent to the owner. The owner came to me for money. He said he needed to pay the electricity. I said I paid my share ,I can't, I have no more money. The owner said the electricity company can be like this. Later we discovered it was the owner who didn't pay the electricity. He just put it in his pocket. Crazy guy. I'm happy that I'm done with that. I have lived Paphos, Nicosia and then I moved to Limassol. Nearly all of Cyprus. I have friends from the North and friends from the South, Turkish-Cypriots and Greek-Cypriots.

But who am I? I was born in the Czech Republic. I can't shake that off. I speak the language I have a passport from there. I guess I have my mentality from there. Now I'm from here. From Cyprus. So, when I travel and someone from the UK asking where I'm from, I say Cyprus. For me, I kinda stopped thinking about countries. Identities. The artificial label we put. What's your path in life? I was born here but then I moved there. So, you're from that country. How is that different from someone who was born here and came there? I don't like borders or boundaries. I like cultures and how they are different. The more different the more pretty, especially when the cultures mix together.'

Like Cyprus. Like Cyprus is trying to become, maybe through a movement of love or maybe through a movement of change. Trying. *For the times they are a-changin'.*[2]

---

2 *Bob Dylan, 'The Times they are A-Changin' (Warner Bros Inc.: 1963, 1964)*

Marriage

I am LARISSA

This koumbaration, this friend network, is so strong and is so widespread here.

She stands peeling carrots and potatoes by the kitchen sink, throwing the skins into one bowl and the undressed vegetables into another. Every so often she glances at the clock and her hand, ripping skin from flesh, moves faster, working up a rhythm, a beat so quick that her hand blurs in motion before finally breaking abruptly to check on the meat, broiling in the cast iron pot over the hob.

'*My poor family is starving today. I didn't prepare a proper lunch for them and this soup will take some time before it is ready*,' she laughs but there are creases in the corners of her eyes, an anxious frown resting on her face. She is a mother who feels with her body the hunger pangs of all her children, husband included. They are all she has, she says, and she grasps them tightly, like the knife in her hand, chopping away at the vegetables, cubing and dicing. Slice.

Her son walks into the kitchen for his morning frappe. The knife is dropped, and instead Larissa moves towards him. She is ready with snack suggestions, hovering over him, her voice a bird that is caught in the breeze. Her son, yawning and scratching the bristles of an emerging beard, merely shrugs. Walks around her. Shuffles through his own movements. Pouring. Stirring. Frothing. Nothing else is of interest to him. The water boils. Coffee powder. Milk. Ice cubes. He ambles back to the living room, coffee in hand, sipping through a straw. The door closes. Larissa turns and almost falls back to the soup, the cutting, the cubing, the dicing.

Larissa first arrived in Cyprus in 1997 and immediately fell in love with the island. It reminded her of Crimea, her beloved hometown, before its economic crisis of the 90s.

'When I first stepped out from the airplane, the air was just like our Crimean air. And I said, "Oh God, thank you!"'

It had not been easy. For two years, Larissa had worked as an au pair in the States, paying off a debt she had accumulated back in Ukraine. She cooked, cleaned, cared for other people's children. At night, she sewed, stitched other children's knee patches, remembering the few minutes of conversation she had snatched with her own child back in Ukraine. That one hour a week was never enough. He was growing up too quickly for her. One birthday after another, one school show after another, another pair of outgrown jeans. Nights, those long long nights were the toughest. At times, the only thing that seemed to keep her from buying the next ticket home (or begging to be sent back) was the thought that soon, very soon, there would be a better life waiting for her in Ukraine. For her, her son, their family. She lived in that hope for two years.

Back in Crimea, however, Larissa's sister had secretly sold Larissa's apartment, leaving the young mother without a roof over her head upon her arrival back in Ukraine. Jobless. With a child clinging to her hand.

Larissa broke down. She felt that she had spent the last two years digging an even larger hole into which to fall.

'When I was left without a home, I just thought to...you know. I called my friends in Moscow out of desperation and they said, "Well, so what? Well, there is no apartment now. Pull your-

self back. There is no point crying about it now, so why worry? Nothing is keeping you there in Crimea, can't you see it is time to leave. Come to Cyprus, we are all resting here, and you should come for a holiday.'"

It was an escape holiday. Unplanned, spur of the moment kind, fleeing from the memorandums Crimea was constantly churning up. She had not chosen Cyprus, for any particular reason, per se.

'What difference did it make to me where to go? If I was told to go to Africa, I would have gone to Africa. I didn't have a home anywhere in the world.'

Larissa and her son's stay extended into a prolonged holiday indeed. Weeks, months went by, and even after their visas had expired, their bags remained unpacked in their small hotel room. Instead, Larissa booked coffee dates with newly-met Russian-speakers, evening dinners at an acquaintance's house, lunch souvlas in the mountains, whole families intact. She rarely had a chance to stop and think what the stamped expiration date on her temporary visitor's visa actually meant.

'I didn't think it was that strict here [regarding visas]. *How could I know? It was '97 and in that year I found out there were a lot of deportations of our Russian girls who were without a visa. One girl, then another girl and another girl. When I finally heard about this, I, of course, started to get very worried and began packing to go back to Ukraine.'*

It was around this time that she met or was forced into an acquaintance with Pavlos Pavlou, a Greek-Cypriot man who turned out to be infatuated with her.

'In the beginning, I didn't even want to know him. But my son said, "Go meet him." I protested, "No, no, I don't want to meet any more Cypriot men."'

But she did. Pavlos was a short, quiet man with kind

brown eyes behind square spectacles and a moustache he had a habit of pulling at the sides when he grew nervous, agitated. When they were together, hie eyes were constantly on Larissa, their softness mellowing into lighter shades whenever she talked, smiled or merely met his gaze.

Larissa did not know a word of Greek, and her English was only slightly better. Pavlos, on the other hand, spoke fluent Russian. During their first meeting, he spoke of how he had recently returned from his university studies in Moscow. His family had always had strong leftist ties growing up. They had been avid supporters of the Communist party of Cyprus from its onset. When an opportunity arose through the launching of a higher education exchange program between Soviet Member States and the Cypriot Communist Party, Pavlos, together with his siblings and classmates, were sent off as the 'first sparrows' to experience the true Soviet life. To become, as he called it, '*sovietised*'.

Within two months, Larissa and Pavlos were living together.

'Pavlos said that he wanted to marry me and on and on. And I said, "How?" At this point, I already had a violation of passport regime. And I didn't know what to do and he said, it doesn't matter, it doesn't matter. We will do it." How should I have known? And he also didn't know. Pavlos, he is like that. He also didn't know all of these dealings. So, we decided to fly back to Ukraine and get married there. Before we left, he collected all the documents here that are needed for marriages abroad, he went around taking oaths on the Bible that he wasn't married and all that. He collected everything, not only collected but translated everything into Russian. All quickly and we thought with these papers everything will go quickly. But when we got to Ukraine, we realised it wasn't that easy to get married to a foreigner. Because he was, of course, a foreigner there. I couldn't get married to

him in Cyprus, I had no visa, no rights there. We got to Ukraine, and we travelled from one end of Ukraine to the other, getting permission here and there, getting more papers, sleeping on the train. It was so difficult. We did it but it was not easy. We signed the papers of our marriage and then almost immediately Pavlos got a call from Cyprus that there was an emergency and we needed to be back immediately. No honeymoon for us, there was no time. We went round changing my passport and to the Cyprus Embassy in Ukraine to get a visa for 30 days for me. There the consular told me I was fine like that, I would just need to go to the Immigration Office when I arrived back in Cyprus and apply for permanent residency.

It sounded easy. It should have been easy.

We arrived at Larnaca airport and walked to Passport Control. They let Pavlos through, no problem, but they stopped me. Pavlos said, "That is my wife!" They, the police, replied, "You go ahead. She is nobody here, nothing to claim here. We will be sending her back!" Pavlos argued, I was in shock. I told Pavlos to go find his brother who worked at the airport. Because he saw us off when we were leaving. I sat there for two hours in the detention room. And Pavlos, he found him, brought him over. The brother went and put down a bribe for me (350 pounds) and only then was I set free. Not because I had a visa or anything. All because of the bribe.

This was '98. That is what was going on around that time.

In the Immigration office they put a stamp in my passport as permanent residency. I was able to work and live. But it took me four years to receive my Cypriot passport. Remember that was before the EU, that was a time when there was a very little queue and Russian wives were getting passports within six months. That was what I had heard. It took me so long because I trusted people.

Pavlos' sister bragged about all her connections (she was in the Communist Party at one point) and said she had a friend that if I gave her my documents, she would give them to him and he would apply for me so that I wouldn't have to go all the way to Nicosia. And I said, "Well, let's do it." So, I gave them to her and that was my mistake. I didn't know what kind of person she was or what she really felt about me. Coming into the family, being the wife of her brother. But slowly she made my life…as painful as she could. My documents disappeared. I believe they were lying around, hidden, in either his (her friend's) or her house for three years. On purpose. Like a hostage. Later, maybe two or three years later, Pavlos' old classmate (he is also a Cypriot) who was in the Left Party from Famagusta asked me whether I had received the Cypriot passport. I said no and he was surprised and said, "But why not?" He started digging and we found out that my name was not even on the list of those who were applying. I would soon learn that this sister was behind this and a lot of other grief in my life. .

But the worst pain in my family's life is the fact that my son does not have residency in this country. He has been here over 20 years now. No passport so no life here in Cyprus, especially now that Cyprus is in the EU. And it is not because of some criminal activity on his part but it reflects how this relative is "helping" us. At first, I didn't take it personally when it was being done towards me. But don't touch my son. I take it personally then. He is a grown man, he has to work to provide for his family. How is he going to do that? He is the son of two Cypriots! Pavlos adopted him and you have to hear about the adoption, you will hear the meddling, all about this "help".

Our application for adoption took five years to finalise. Five years! Pavlos does not have any children and it is obvious he will not have any now. We are not at that age. We'd hoped to have children but it never happened.

One day, Pavlos had come up to my son and had asked him,

"Do you want to be my son?" My son said, "Yes I do". They had kept it private at first, it was something between them. They told me only later when they decided to apply for an official adoption, even though my son was over eighteen. It was a very long process. But we were patient. The representative of the government befriended us, she would come over for coffee, call up. I thought she liked us. But what I have learned in Cyprus is to trust no one but your close family.

During the last court case, well, before it began, I sat with that representative of the government, having a tête-à-tête. Very friendly. I remember she was telling an anecdote and I was laughing. My lawyer approached and asked to speak with me in private for a moment. All in whispers, the lawyer said, "What are you doing speaking with the devil?"

I was shocked. But she continued, "You are talking with that woman but do you know how many nails in your tires she has placed, so to speak. How many lies and insults she has fired against you to the judge. Don't you know that the decision of the court is due to her 'helpful' input?"

"Decision of the court?"

"Your application has been rejected."

"But we haven't even made our last case… On what grounds rejected?"

"You will have to ask her. She must have something against you for her to be pushing the judge this hard so he would reject your application even before the hearing."

I was shocked, I was really really shocked. There was nothing to do about it but one thing and it was the only chance. I was in tears when I found my husband. And I told him what I had heard and then I said to him, "If you don't speak up now for your son and for yourself, you will always regret it. It was your initiative to adopt him. I never asked you, this is something you and my son decided together. Please, don't stay quiet." When we enter the courthouse, and the court is in session, that woman starts attacking us, saying that the only reason my son wanted to be adopted is to get the passport but the passport (Cyprus was already in the EU at this point) was not a reason for adoption, we were just abusing the system etc. When did we ever say that? She had met my husband, she knew his feelings towards my son. At that point, for the first time, Pavlos stood up. The judge asked if he has something to say.

"Do you have kids?" he asked the judge.

"Yes."

"Well, I don't. Nor will I have any. I love this woman. We live together already 18 years. I know this boy for 18 years, I want him to be my son. I want to leave him everything when I pass away. I did not come to ask your permission but for the paperwork. He will be my son. If you will reject me now I will go further to the EU Court."

It was the first time I really saw Pavlos shout. He was angry. But he was also very sad.

"You have kids. Don't you want your last glass to be brought by your children? I want that, just as I did for my own father. Why are you taking this right from me? This is my decision and I should be the one deciding whether I should do this or not. Passport or not, he is my son and you have no right to deny me my wish."

After my husband spoke, he saw me crying. Everyone in that room was moved, I know for sure. But that woman, that heartless… (excuse my language), just wouldn't let go of what she had against us. She was still pressing on and on. She even started saying that because we hadn't yet paid our lawyer, we should be rejected. What has that got to do with the application?

I knew there had to be something behind her sudden hate for us. And I found out later there was. It turns out she was an old friend of that "helpful" relative of ours. She was returning a fa-

vour or was blackmailed, I don't know. But she was doing all she could to make our life miserable so that woman, that "relative", would be happy. That relative would go so far as to tell everyone, all her acquaintances in Immigration, in the Ministries, Law Courts, wherever I knocked for my son, that I had married Pavlos for a passport, for money (what money?!), and other horrible, disgusting things that she spread in all the right offices. All lies! But she hated me and wanted me to suffer. Maybe she just didn't trust me? I don't know.

If I were to come to you and tell you to not help this one person because she is like this and that, you would listen to me. You know me, we have a good relationship, so you would believe me. Because I am your koumbaros, your friend, relative. Not a stranger. Rather than the stranger who comes to you and asks for help. I understand this. But I am a bit of a different type of person. I don't listen to the opinion of others. My opinion forms from how I see our relationship developing. If this person asks me to help them, I will. I won't listen to the opinions of others.

But in Cyprus, unfortunately, they listen. It's right, on the one hand, but only if the other person is telling the truth. What if it is a bunch of lies?

This koumbaration, this friend network, is so strong and is so widespread here. I know for sure it is responsible for stopping my son from ever acquiring Cypriot citizenship. Recently, he was put on the stop list for no reason, almost arrested and deported. If he was deported, it would be forever. I would never see him again. Because somebody has a serious grudge against me and she has the power of connections. To destroy me and my family.

What is this? What are these laws that anybody can just come and influence the decision to change someone's life? To make them go away? In Cyprus, they can. This is the biggest problem in Cyprus. This koumbaration. The European Union promises to bring families together but Cyprus is breaking families apart. If they would at least listen to the truth. My husband and I have been living together twenty-one years now. We are happy. If we weren't, he would have left years ago. How can they believe the lies? But they were told something black, and that is how it is: black. Despite this island being so welcoming, this racism…'

She puts the knife down. There is a smell of burning. The meat. Quickly, she pours more liquid into the pot and stirs the bone, the flesh floating one way and the other, round and round, as if caught in a whirlwind, round and round, and round and round, and there is another smell, the spices, round and round, but still a hint of that burning flesh, mixed with everything else, round and round the room. And then she stops. Larissa drops the spatula on a plate by the stove and comes round to sit by me for a bit. Tired, eyes wet, her lips tasting the broth that she herself does not understand anymore.

'Почему?' she asks, 'Why?'

I am ZUZANA

The Immigration office acts as the face of the Government, and this face is hideous.

I was born by the Baltic Sea, in the city of Ventspils, during the Communist era. From my father's line, they are Latvian with Germanic roots and on my mother's side they are Hungarian-Finnish. This is why we are all strange, our physiognomy. Mine especially. I don't look German nor Russian nor Latvian. I look more northern, more Finnish. Mixed blood.

To be honest, I pity the current generation. We had free everything: schools, after school activities, and food, four times a day. We were always busy with something. Dancing, music, swimming, astronomy, physics, wood crafting, athletics, art, camping trips. Everything was to the full. It was safe. The understanding of don't go there in case someone does something, we just didn't have that. Maybe there were things but it didn't touch us kids. That fear that we have now wasn't there.

Yes, we had a coupon system and I remember standing with my coupons in a queue. But you know what we didn't have? This consumerism. Going to the shops, buying by sight only and then throwing half the things out of your fridge. That we didn't have. This is Cyprus. This understanding that if you have filled your fridge to the brim, then it is a mark of your wealth, and half the things aren't eaten but thrown away. There weren't any shops but everyone had butter, everyone had salt and sugar, bread, kolbasa cuts and cheese. We had canned fish products since we were by the sea, canned meat, all this we could buy however much you wanted but not in the same way like here. You gave your coupon, got your products and you had enough. You ate economically because you understood you don't have the choice to throw things away. There was a calculated ratio for each individual and it was enough because when the coupon system dissolved, people started buying washing-up products, soap, bread, alcohol (in Yeltsin's era). People had these but they would just lie around, or people would resell them or give them away. Cigarettes were resold because they just weren't being used. But this greediness of just to own, this was not present. Everyone had a different relationship with these material things.

My dad died when I was 6 years old, so my mum raised me by herself. Mostly. She worked two jobs even while I was still quite young. I learnt to be independent because she had to leave before I was off for school. And school was a few kilometers away. I walked by myself there and back. Every morning and afternoon, all year round. Kids are spoilt now compared to what I had to do. My day went something like this. Early in the morning, Mum would be off for her 8am shift by bus. I learnt to do pigtails early in my life, although mum sometimes would wake me so she could do them for me before she left. I'd then get myself ready without her, feed the cats, go for water at the well, lock the door. Sometimes I wouldn't see mum the whole week. When I'd come home from school, she'd be away working. So, I would change my clothes, do a bit of homework, have some lunch, wash after myself, take care of the cats, and be off to music classes where I played the violin. I would only be home at 8pm, 8.30pm, and I'd be coming to an empty house again as mum was usually already at the theatre on her second shift. I guess you could say it was lonely but the system was set up that we were surrounded with people all day. But still. How shall I sum it up? We survived. But, honestly, I had a great childhood.

Of course, I grew up in a very different culture to that in which I live in now. Our Latvian culture was about respect.

We built houses at a distance from everyone else. Unlike here in Cyprus where they live on top of each other and look into each other's windows. Everyone needs to know the business of their neighbours. There were no gates or fences. Maybe around the garden to protect it from pests such as deer, rabbits or around the cows and sheep to protect them from wolves but then it would be corrugated wire. A fence to mark out territory was an unknown phenomena. The mentality of everyone for themselves is hard to get used to. We respected each other's privacy and we didn't need special reinforcement to remind others of that respect. That is important because when I came to Cyprus, it was then that I realised how disrespectful they are and how unique this Latvian, Baltic, culture is.

Anyway, I finished school and I decided that I wanted to work in the police force. I had this dream to become a lawyer but then I warmed to a more military profession. And I didn't want to go to the army. I ended up working for the gorkom, the City Committee of the Communist Party of the Soviet Union. I had grown up in a town where there was a cosmic unit on one end, military bases all around and the headquarters of the spy satellite in the woods. Now I was working beside them. Let me tell you, this was a completely different level of people. I was the youngest there from all four floors, people would blow sawdust from my shoulders as the saying goes. Next to us were the headquarters of the KGB. We would have lunch with them in the dining hall. Even today people don't believe how close I was to the KGB, how much time I spent near them, talking to them. After the gorkom, they promoted me to the Komsomol, The All-Union Leninist Young Communist League. That was a different scale. The most unpleasant duty of the job was presenting medals to parents of deceased soldiers, the boys who were 17 or 18 at most. You cannot imagine what I had to go through emotionally to get the job done. But I worked and I became friends with so many people in different quarters of life. I would talk to millionaires, criminals with a very dark record, and you don't realise how simple they both are, always speaking in a low tone, with respect, slowly. Imagine the position I was in there and nobody ever raised their voice against me.

But here in Cyprus, oh there is so little respect. They talk like morons. I remember one incident (I will never forget it) this bastard made me, a grown woman, cry. Not because he hurt me but because the Cypriot is a fully-fledged idiot himself, crude, no manners and I have little faith in his intellectual capacity. I was at a lawyer's office and this so-called lawyer had just been talking to someone on the phone. Someone had just called him about something or other, and I happened to be walking in there. And he turns to me with a "GET OUT". Absolutely out of his mind yelling. No apologies, no greeting to the new client walking into your office. I was stunned. Understand this, how could I, with how I grew up, know how to react? For somebody to try to fling you out the door, shout as if he were in flames, just because your lover has just let slip to your wife about the after work affair, or you didn't get what you wanted, and like a child you took it out on a complete stranger, is just…it's just all screwed up.

But maybe Cypriots are used to this instead of a hello but me, no I am not. I cried but the crying was not weakness, it's just a reaction to the shame he put on me because who was this person? Nobody. A nobody! I'd understand if he was some big shot, with titles and honours, with a real name, but of course these type of people don't allow themselves to react in this way. They are of a different caliber. They hold themselves together. There is business and there is the personal and then there is what is inside you. Keep it separate. Here is a lesson for these types of people like this so-called 'lawyer'.

It took me a long time to get over this incident. I remember walking out of the office, turning around to the management and saying, "If you don't remove this person from your office, you will not have any clients. The way he treats people is disgraceful. How can you call yourself a business enterprise with such a lawyer?" Can you just imagine him in court if the Judge doesn't rule in his favor, or with other clients? Can you imagine him with sensitive cases? I feel sorry for anybody who ends up with him.

But for them it's all OK, everyone's a koumbaros, all a bunch of…Excuse me but it's true. In my culture, people understand that beyond black and white there are other tones to consider. I was taught to not react to these kinds of people. No yelling back, putting up the finger, with a great 'Reeeeee!', whilst driving like crazy along the street. I'm not like them.

No, never.

But no, wait. I do that now. Oops, yes I did it the other day. Oh. Cyprus has taught me well.

But back to my story. After Komsomol, I got married, started a business, had children, got divorced. The usual. I had numerous incidents of foreign men who knew my connections, "my people" I called them, asking to marry me for the Soviet passport. Legally, they couldn't offer me monetary compensation but through marriage, really all under the table, they were offering me everything. "You will live however you like, my home will be yours." They were from former Yugoslavia, and it was a luxurious place back then. Their houses were like mansions. Even now I think how life would've turned out if I'd said yes. Maybe not how they painted it what with all the wars that came later. But it's nice to think I could have had it all. Oh well.

Then Independence came for us Latvians and everything turned to trash. It was then that we had starvation. Not what all these history books try to sell you. Nearly thirty years after proclaiming their Independence, the Latvians still have the vulgarity to blame the Russians for their own mistakes. Latvians couldn't and still can't govern a country. The Russians have nothing to do with Latvian incompetence. It was the Latvian's fault for our mess of a life during that time.

That was the country and, of course, everyone was affected. I ran up to threats against my own business. Latvia was a hole of corruption and thieves, maybe still is. But those "questions" used to be solved quickly and quietly. Nobody used to touch me, or my business. They knew I was still in good relations with people of high status in the criminal world. And also in the police force. Sometimes, I was even the mediator between them. Those people who had been working for the KGB (the ones I met over lunch when I was working for the Komsomol) went every which way in the country post-Independence, bad and good, whatever those are, and they needed someone to keep the peace between them.

For me, I needed to survive and so did my children. I had a license for a pistol, my own private gunfire. I used to carry it around everywhere. But then I had to give it up because my husband (ex) submitted a statement that I was trying to kill him with it (if I really wanted to shoot him, I would have, I had good aim). But it just shows what kind of stuff men are made of.

My husband made my life hell after the divorce. He told me he'd never let me live life freely. So much dirt and mess. It was a nightmare. He didn't pay any child support and I practically raised two kids on my own. But he kept trying to squeeze more out of me, more and more. We were constantly in court, whenever he would run out of money. I remember he would even come over to my flat on the pretext to visit the children but really it was to cut a piece a bread from our loaf to take home with him. Instead of bringing something for the children, he was cutting from their portion for himself. Within a few years, I was ready to give up. If my son, I used to think to myself, was to ever grow up like his father, that would be my end. It was then that I'd convinced myself I needed to get out of there, him especially, from out of the shadow of that man.

I was tired. From the business. From Latvia and its god-damn Russia-hating patriotism. From the years of stress and struggle. My husband had robbed me well throughout that year and I was having to pay off massive debts because of him. I was just not interested any more. With no money left in the bank to feed my children. I was shattered and deeply depressed.

Just at that time an opportunity came up. My sister had moved to Cyprus earlier and married a Syrian. So, I also came over. I needed a break and she paid for my ticket. And I met someone. He was from Sri Lanka. He was my way out to get out of Latvia, run away from my ex-husband. Yes, he had a very different background, different religion but he was more Buddhist. I could deal with that. He'd been brought over from Dubai by a Cypriot to work at a large hotel in Paphos. He was a chef, a real professional at his job. He was in very good relations, he and his boss. How do I say this? An opportunity because we had an agreement about what this arrangement would mean. Our marriage that is. I knew I had to leave, rescue my children. This man helped save them. And save myself. He brought me out of the darkness that I was in at that point of my life by giving me the opportunity to move to Cyprus. I finally had hope. Yes, you can say he changed his status because he married a European passport, that in a way he was the winning party of our union. That he benefitted. He had big problems with visa applications and he had to step over that hurdle. As someone from a third world country, he was only allowed to stay in Cyprus for maximum five years (with his visa renewed yearly of course) and when we met it was his eighth year. The Immigration was doing everything to kick him out even though his employer was pleading to have him stay. But we both took something, it was an equal transaction. It was not a light task to bring me out of that country and he paid for everything. They call it fake but how? There was a contract like in every marriage and we both fulfilled our parts. He wanted to work in this country. How is that criminal?

Let me tell you something about the Immigration office. It acts as the face of the Government, and this face is hideous. Everybody who has had to go through Immigration has seen its ugly, sexist, racist face. The corruption there is unbelievable. The people visiting it there shamelessly, clutching their bribes, walk into the director's office. He happily lets them through and voilà their papers are ready the next day. And we, my husband and I, saw huge stacks of money on the director's desk with a list of ticked names on top. I swear this is true. Everyone around here knows that the Immigration Office abides by its own law. Now my husband refused to bribe, I can vouch for that. He was very serious about his principles. This is why the Immigration Office did everything in their power to make him leave the island. He was due to apply for citizenship but the Office didn't want a Sri Lankan to get a Cypriot passport. Wouldn't even let him remain on a working visa despite his having all the correct paperwork. Racists!

We were forced to appeal to the Supreme Court. And there even the judge was confused. He said, "I have no idea what spectacle the Immigration Office is trying to flaunt in my face. The man is legal here. Legal! Social Insurance paid? Paid. Who is he married to? EU. Why are you not giving him the Yellow Slip, permanent residency? What's this about not even giving him the Pink Slip, the temporary visa for one year? They are married so he should automatically be granted at least that." The Immigration Officer was furious in that court room. Red in the face, making excuses. I can't even remember the excuses. We won the case, of course. But at what cost?

As revenge, the Immigration Office sent me a letter. A week later it was. This letter said that if I, a European national, didn't leave Cyprus within the next 20 days, the authorities will deport me. That I was abusing the Cypriot system because I married a

Sri Lankan. That I, a European, was not allowed to marry a Sri Lankan, apparently. Racist bastards! How was that even allowed in a European country?

My life was a scene from Romeo and Juliet. The irony, yes? The greatest love story and then there is me and him. I was arrested and spent time in prison. We both did. My husband and I sat there behind bars. That was a real moment, a real test of character. We were friends and that tested our friendship really hard. We went through so much together, it is unbelievable. He had been so loyal to me, to the Cyprus government. A model citizen. And look how they treated him. Disgusting!

My husband asked for divorce as he saw that was the only way out. He was deported but, he was such a good man, he saved me again. I was allowed to stay in Cyprus. You have to understand, maybe it wasn't a normal marriage but it was a friendship. We never tried to do something to hurt anyone. We just wanted to live, to find a little joy in life. Somewhere.

Cyprus wouldn't even give us that.

What can I say, yes, I stayed here. I have lived here for eleven years now. I have made friends, I have made enemies. But they are not going to kick me out, no, they have tried to but they forget who they are dealing with. I cried once because a Cypriot man dared raise his voice but that was because I was off my guard. Now I am ready to hit back. I will just give them a great big, "Reeeeeeeeeee!" and we will see this woman standing on top. There you go, don't forget that picture. Write it down for yourself.'

I am BIRYAR

Words they can't change anything big.
Maybe give some to feel happy sometimes.

'What matters in life is not what happens to you but what you remember and how you remember it,' writes Gabriel García Márquez in the first volume of his autobiographical work, *Living to Tell the Tale.* This is how I would like to remember Biryar. Through quotes, a writer writing on writers, a writer living among, through and with other writers (spiritually, of course). Biryar is a writer of short stories, poems, and articles. He breathes and eats words just as he does a plate of souvla over the weekend with his Greek Cypriot parents-in-law. Pulling a chunk from its skewer, cutting into the still smoke-hot meat, that bite, juices seeping from the corners of his lips, chin and dripping down, whilst strands of meat are caught between teeth. Then comes the sense of taste, yes salt, yes oregano, yes yes pepper. Slowly, there is a murmur, the sound of 'Mmmmmmm'.

'I'm Kurdish from Syria.'

There are approximately 1.7 million Kurds currently residing in Syria, predominantly in the northern regions that border with Turkey. Despite their small numbers (in comparison to their numbers in Turkey, Iraq and Iran), the community remains the largest ethnic minority group in Syria. At the collapse of the Ottoman Empire and the end of World War I, the Kurds were offered an autonomous homeland through the Treaty of Sevres. Nevertheless, the promises were never acted upon. The new Turkish government replaced the latter treaty with one of their own, that of the 1923 Treaty of Lausanne and, therefore, the Kurds were never granted a place to call home. In consequence, the ethnic minority has been a victim to severe discrimination and political oppression in the hands of the Syrian government.

'I didn't come by airport to Larnaca. No, this is a different story. In Syria, Kurdish people, half of them do not have nationality. No rights. They are aliens. We are aliens in our country. They don't give nothing. Maybe this make me to don't feel there is place that is my country. Maybe.'

During a census collection in October 1962, Syrian authorities denied registration to approximately 150,000 Kurds in the Hassaka region. No conclusive reasoning behind their decision was offered. As a result, these individuals and their descendants became and remain stateless within the territory. *Aliens.* Without the correct documents, they are refused basic human rights. For instance, they are not permitted to vote, own property or even practice their culture or language. In fact, the use of the Kurdish dialect, Kurmaji, is forbidden, though it is still spoken at home by the community. However, in March 2004, as a result of frustration at the ongoing oppression and false promises of the new president in regards to the Kurds, protests, or 'intifada' (uprising), broke out, encouraged by the demonstrations by their Kurdish brothers in nearby Iraq. In response, the Syrian government, took severe measures to suppress collective gatherings, or even the possibility for the occurence of collective gatherings, whether political, cultural or social. Those engaging in organised activism would be arrested under the state's Emergency Law of 1963. Torture, physical and mental abuse, are not uncommon for incarcerated suspects. Against a community seeking only recognition and respect, in response the state has called a war of hate, fear and violence.

Biryar sits opposite me as day begins to give way to the dimness of evening. He has come straight from work, a long strenuous day. His mind seems to be elsewhere at times, possibly musing over what his wife may be doing at that very moment, his children. Maybe he should squeeze in a short writing session before bed. He hides a yawn with the back of his hand. Maybe not.

'I never think to be a patriot. I feel like a man who live once. No borders. Whenever you leave, you feel that. If you feel good, it's your country wherever. The Kurdish situation was no good. That's why I decided to leave Syria. I needed papers. I wanted to go to my relatives in Germany and Sweden but the situation was difficult so I say we go Cyprus. We went to special people, we found two people. They took us to the other side of Cyprus, the Turkish side, and then you know…it wasn't legal. I didn't want any problems with Cypriot people because when I see them, I have communication with them. In my opinion, they belong to the Middle East, not Europe. Even their food, their ways to live. Everything. And they are so close to us. That make it easy for me to work with them and to live with them. From the first moment I came to this country, I didn't get any help from government. I work with my hands and I get money. Without anything, even sin. Look, until you can't work, why you ask? There is people who need help, they (the government) *should help them first, and then we will see.'*

His gestures are definitive like full stops. He guards his emotions, especially when asked about how he feels about leaving his family back in Syria. Those emotions, they have passed, he whispers. If not, there would never have been Cyprus.

'I start work immediately for Cypriots when I come. I speak

a little bit of English, I teach myself, and they want workers. I give them what they want and they give me what I want. I need money to live here. A job. I didn't know Greek. Nothing nothing nothing, even worse. My neighbour, who become my friend, he teach me. He decide, he ask me to teach him Arabic and he teach me Greek. I learn Greek but he never learn Arabic because I speak Arabic.

I marry. My wife, I work with her father and I saw her. This way. We love each other. The parents were not happy at first. At They were afraid. They say, this in not Cypriot. Maybe he will not be a good man. Maybe he run. I don't marry for papers, I tell them. Slowly slowly they know me, they love. We come together and make souvlaki, souvla. First in Cyprus is food. Souvla, koupepia, makaronia tou fournou. I cook also. Syrian food is no different but they like salt too much here. I don't like salt. My mother-in-law she put salt. "Vale, Vale", put, put, all the time.

Now my wife and me, we have children. We send them to school and now we send them to learn English. Till this moment, I've had no nationality of any kind. No passport. That's why my kids, I didn't teach them my language. We speak Greek at home. They know some words in Arabic. I say, let them learn English first. If they want to learn my language, they will learn it. Let them grow up, slowly slowly. My language is not international language. My sister is an English teacher. We speak on Skype. She speak with my wife but my kids can't speak English yet. They know some words, "How are you? How are you?" but, ahhhhh, they struggle.

About language. You know I wrote a poem about this. If you speak your language good you will speak the other language when you learn it. Every English man has his dictionary of English. He will not use all of the words that English has. But me as an example. I speak my language good, Kurdish, Arabic. Two languages 100%. I learn Greek, I learn English. My English maybe not too good but my Greek is better. I forget French, je ne sais pas, because like music, if you don't use it, you lose it. But I have my languages and now I have more languages. Beautiful.

I read in Arabic. I write in Kurdish and Arabic. In 2002, I published my first book in Kurdish. In Syria. Why do I write? I don't know. It's like why you eat? To continue our life. Because there is book, there must be someone who read that book. I don't write to change the whole world, nobody can change the whole world. Maybe Trump. Power. Power of words. Never change anything. I hope to change something, something small. Write something for all people for the country you live in. But it's difficult. Words, they can't change anything big. Maybe give some to feel happy sometimes. Power, wars change the world. I come from war, it change me.'

It is getting late. Bats are speckling the night sky, flashing across the darkness of the street. The street is busy with the headlights of cars, the blast of radios, that week's International Top Hit. Biryar is finishing the last of his coffee and we are just about to head our separate ways when he offers a last thought.

'I read Chekov. In one story, it about man who, you know 100 years ago have no cars. Just horse and cart. This man son has died. So this man want to talk to someone to feel that someone share his pain. He want to speak. All the people who came with him, his passengers, he told them his story. But nobody tried to learn what happened with him. No one wants to hear so he speaks to his horse. Short story that nobody listen to you when you have problems… maybe I don't agree but he writes like this. You can't change it.'

I am BELLA

You are in this country,
you have to adapt.

'Do not allow the dissolution of any marriage. Bless, Lord, all couples. Make them be mystically united in the bond of sincere love and in the sacrament, just as Christ, the Bridegroom, is with his Bride, the Church.' (Marriage Liturgy)

It was kind of the minister to read a translation of his blessings to the newlyweds, a sympathetic gesture towards the bride who, being from abroad, had not understood a word of his service, executed in Ancient and Modern Greek. She was young, with long locks curling in small waves along her back, like the afternoon sea come September. There she was, standing before him, her eyes gleaming, opaque pools, clear blue water of excitement. *This is the day, my day, I've been dreaming about. The day everything changes, the day everything comes true.* She would later describe that day as the eve and slow end to her naiveté. A death dressed in white. Because it all began with the dress.

'I didn't do it on purpose. It was perfectly natural for me to want something like that, to be like that, I didn't think that it would shock. But they had never seen anything like it.'

They had not. It was the fashion of the metropolises of Europe, the feature of all the big magazines, the fashion shows of Paris, Milan. An off-white piece that dived v-shaped at the front, exposing a little too much for the kind minister's wandering eye, with an open back, an oval of exposed pale skin, just slightly caressed by the summer's rays.

There was lace, tight tight lace and a long tail. There was no taking your eyes off of her, no stopping your staring at the beautiful body beneath that dress.

Which was, of course, a problem for the conservative Greek Orthodox groom's family. They had not expected she would choose that dress. The mother-in-law especially. Even after the first few clack clack clacks of the heels on marble, the chorus of gasps and snorts, even after the murmurs of those waking up from a trance after seeing *that* dress in *their* church (*Blasphemy!*) breathing again after seeing so much skin (*showing so much…there!*), even then it was hard to believe. The mother-in-law had purposely directed and dictated almost every detail of the wedding, so that no foreignness could slip into *her* son's event. And now this! How did this happen? What will the neighbours think? What were they thinking just then?

It had all began with that dress. That foreign dress.

The streets of Limassol were an ugly place for a foreign woman, day or night. The air was hot and clammy with 'Haaaaalooooo', 'Haaaaaaalooooo', 'Haaaaaalooooo' from passing vehicles, or from the man across the street. Then there were the comments thrown out of Mercedes cars like cigarette butts, jeering, taunting, threatening. A walk was never just a walk. There was always something that happened.

Upon Bella's first arrival on the island, walks were a daily habit. Maybe it was the sea, the winding streets, or even the small bustle of life in what she first considered to be a sleeping village. But soon she began to resent going out. She could not stand the whistles and laughter, those hand gestures. They would always make a big deal of her foreigness, make her feel smaller, ashamed.

'I couldn't wear shorts because then I couldn't walk down the street. It was something that was really suffocating for me. I mean it was perfectly normal for me back from where I grew up for a young lady to wear shorts. It was nothing unusual. I realised here if I was walking down the street on my own, and dressed like this, it would be an unending story. Men weren't behaving. Maybe because they didn't see a lot of tourists until then. There were a lot of Swedish, Danish at the time, but still just for holiday. It wasn't the time when a lot of foreigners had settled in Cyprus yet. So, it was something unusual for that, both in the family and for strangers. I had to adjust. The trousers came, the longer skirts, the longer sleeves. And then I started to breathe a little bit. Some people say, why do you change yourself, you shouldn't have to. That is my experience. I believe you have to make some adjustments. It can't all be one way, you can't expect the whole world to change and you remain the same. You are in this country, you have to adapt. To a certain extent, I am not saying change completely and not be who you are anymore because whatever happens outside, you will still remain who you are. A piece of cloth doesn't really make that much difference.'

This was the beginning of a series of alterations Bella would make as she adjusted to life in Cyprus. The woman, the wife, the domestic servant, the prudent, the quiet, the outsider. The *paraxenoi* woman, strange in all her ways. She dressed and was dressed in all these new names that had come with marrying into a Greek-Cypriot family and then living on the island. This was the '*big village*' culture of Cyprus of that period, where '*everybody was in everybody's business*'. She knew that she was the topic of gossip, the subject of long debates in kitchens and on porches. Every step she took called for scrutiny. Neighbours spent hours mourning over the good old days when 'our' men didn't look at foreign women, tsk-tsking over these 'xenoi kopeles', these foreign girls of no modesty, no religion, no honor? Bella knew she was watched, she felt the eyes of the whole town upon her at every breath of the day in the first few years.

Even Bella's partner had to change, leaving his UK ways behind, almost into somebody his new wife could not recognise.

'He was like a different man. I was like, what is going on here?'

At first, he had appeared passive about Bella taking on a job, but soon this changed.

'There was an enormous amount of jealousy on the part of my husband, which led me to stop that job. I had to quit because of the pressure I felt always when I was out, oh this one he talks to you, the other he talks to you, you know. And I felt, I mean we were just engaged, we were about to get married, I don't want this kind of atmosphere. At the time I felt anything to keep the peace. If there was an evening without the spouses, without the husbands or whatever, just the office staff, which used to happen sometimes or a lunch or something, I always used to find it extremely difficult. He just couldn't get used to it, he just couldn't take it, he was continually afraid and very jealous. Oh boy, was I stunned. So that was the first time that I saw something wrong here but then at the time things weren't like they are now, where a woman would really fight to get her rights. It was more like slowly slowly. And you must do as you are told.'

Her life was then confined to the house, the long days, the loneliness that permeated the evenings, waiting for her husband to return from his office parties and after-work drinks. But it soon became clear that the changes did not stop there.

'When we were going somewhere, the men were sitting with the men, the women with the women. Everything was like natural spread. It was some things we talk to the women about, some things we don't talk to the women about. The first time I was very surprised was when we were at the table, at the sister's house, and the mother had cooked everything, and we were sitting. And I heard, "Mana to psomi", "Mother, the bread". His mother would have to get up to go and get the bread, the mother who is older than the one who spoke, her already grown-up child, she, the mother, who just cooked, and I am thinking why doesn't that person get up to get the bread? It was not please, mother can I have the bread? Where did you put the bread? "Mana to psomi." Not even her name, but Mana.'

As the days, weeks, months passed, without the cushion of her own family to fall back on, the foreign woman was alone in the battle against what she saw as an outdated system, patriarchy she had thought she had long left behind in the village where she had been raised. Alone but not entirely the only one in a similar situation.

'Somebody I became friends with who was from Switzerland a few years later she divorced, she left. A lot divorced, women like this. They could not take this.'

It was kind of the minister to read a translation of his blessing. Bella still remembers the words. If everything else appeared bleak and dim, those words would always fill her heart with a story. A happy ending. There is something in that.

Dad

I am BORA

Who do I want to be? Somebody who can stand up for those I love...

'It is what it is.'

'My mum is Cypriot, grew up in a village. Troulloi. OG like that. I think it is one of the villages in the UN buffer zone, not that it means much if you are there. Mum was born and raised there, I was born and raised there. My father was born and raised in Turkey. In a village called Uşak. So ,they are both kinda villagers from different countries.

I visited Uşak a while back. It was like going back in time. A very lawful lawless place. Everyone is very nice but, if someone does something bad, they get shot. If anything happens there, the closest to anything, any hospitals, doctors, even the basics like supermarkets and stuff, is like 100km away so they have to kinda look after themselves. Everyone is super welcoming and polite but they have no room for any strange things, any dangers to themselves, like rapists or anything. So, naturally the village there must be cleansed of these people. Although, from what I hear, nothing much ever happens there. It is beautiful, everyone just raising their animals. It is different to Cyprus where you are used to a village being like five houses and ten minutes by car from everything. There it took four hours to get to that village, it was horrifying. There were wolves everywhere. My dad's best friend told me that the next time I came, I can go shepherd with him. He goes on a tractor in the middle of the night with a pistol and kind of just looks after the animals. Protecting them from the wolves. Gives me the creeps.

You can imagine that such a village is not the scene for some people. Gets boring, ties you down a bit. That was my dad. He was one of the first Turks to come over here to Cyprus after the 1974 war. Dad was a bit, not ahead of his time, but he didn't want to stay in Turkey. He wanted his own freedom, he wanted to be his own man. So he said, Let me go to this island and see what's up. Dad probably knew kind of what happened in the invasion but he probably didn't pay attention to it. Somehow, he came through Greece. You can imagine how popular he was here in the beginning. He was deported a couple of times. Dad was very hands on you could say. Like he had to put a couple of people away, not kill them but he had to fight them. This was the 80s and it was not like he could turn to the police force for help. Dad was vulnerable, but he was also dangerous. Because where he grew up, it was life or death. It didn't help that there were frictions with people and things like that. You know someone says something to you and you have to defend yourself or you end up…It's a blood thing. So, dad was kind of OK, obviously the cops were in his ass. They beat him up once. The cops ganged up on him. I had a friend whose dad was a cop and the dad once said to me, "I remember your dad, he was in one of the cells." They even made an article about him in the newspaper that my dad still has to this day. They called him the "Terror of Cyprus". Which some is warranted, I'll admit, because dad has a no bull shit policy. But, terror, really?

So, dad came over, started working for this guy who owned a slaughterhouse and gradually he was able to take a job as a butcher in a supermarket in Larnaca. That's where he met my mother. Their "meat story". He barely spoke Greek, barely barely spoke Greek. She knew someone who kind of spoke Turkish and somehow they were able to communicate. I guess when mum saw him she was like, "he has nice meat", or something. It was not romantic, he was being cheesy but this was in the late 80s, so of course it was going to be cheesy.

Mum's family reacted in the worst way. I mean, you can understand them. Her parents went through the war. Think of what a disgrace it was. Their daughter marrying a Turk. Know what I mean? What is the family going to say, what are people going to say? Nobody was happy. Matter of fact my grandmother was like, I don't want you having a child with this man. Because she feared he was going to run away. You have to understand these are old people who know this one way of life. They are not intentionally racist, it's all they know. It was tough. But they took it, you know, they loved her. I think the one who took it the hardest was my uncle who was almost promoted to be the chief of police but never became that because his sister married a Turk. He was very bitter then.

I grew up divided between town and village where my grandma lived. I applaud that woman (my grandmother) because she raised a Turkish kid, took that burden on herself and still loved me. I was happy with her, I never lacked anything, I was well fed, well taken care of. My grandmother had my back. But it wasn't easy, I'll tell you that. The rest of the village just hated me because I was the son of the Turk. You know what I mean? Cypriot village after the invasion. Less than 20 years. I knew these people hated me for my dad, it was what it was. I had to be cautious where I went. I was technically allowed to go wherever I wanted but I would get beat up by the kids all the time. The adults encouraged it. There was no logic in their ways, there was only prejudice. I understand prejudice in people who were in the war but you are asking children to hate another child that has nothing to do with anything. My father was not in the war. My father was in a village in the middle of nowhere and he barely knew where Cyprus was. They were just telling these kids to hate me. And it worked.

People threw explosives into the yard, when they knew I was playing there. So, they lobbed them hoping to get me. One landed right next to my face but, in God's grace, it didn't go off. In scouts in Troulloi, I was on the bus and this girl comes up behind me, clips my legs and I fall face first. And no one helped me, everyone was stepping over me or on me as they were getting off the bus. I remember like it was yesterday. The scout leaders did nothing. What are they going to do? It's a Turkish guy, they don't care. Matter of fact they may have stepped on me too, I don't know. That was bullshit because at the end of the day I was still a child. If you look inside and look at what is going on over here, you realise you are hurting a child and they were just OK with it.

I did one year of primary school in Troulloi before they had to take me out. I was getting attacked everywhere. People would beat me up and run away. That was like a thing in Troulloi. I was like a drive-by. It was crazy. I was run over. My father actually left the country and wouldn't actually have come back. He was like, I'm done with this shitplace. The law was awful and he was like I am done. My mum went anorexic and she died for a bit, her heart stopped. I was too young to think about it. And then one day I was running down this slope so you couldn't really see me. Dad thinks it was planned but I don't know. I remember running and then I remember being under a car. So, I was run over and that is the only reason he came back. He was like, they are going to kill my son. So, that was the incident that started everything like a chain reaction. Dad left everything there in Turkey and came back just to make sure I was going to be OK. And man if he'd never come back, I don't think I would be here today.

That was till I was eight and then I was moved to a school in Larnaca. Things didn't improve much. And my dad really had to step in. I had teachers refusing to teach me when I was younger and dad got them fired. He once beat the shit out of a kid in front of his parents. Slapped him around and then he told the parents, "You make a move and I will kill you right here."

Let me explain. This kid almost killed me. He threw me down the stairs and I am not talking a few steps, these were those cracked staircases you get in public schools where each step is death with one wrong move. I went to the office to explain to them what happened and, get this, the principal almost congratulated the kid for doing that. So, when I told my dad what happened he was fucking furious.

Another time, this kid beat me up, really bad, bad enough I had to call my dad to come pick me up. Dad then waited outside the school for this kid and dad was like, "Is that him?" As the kid was running home, Dad literally drove next to him slapped him on the back of his head and the kid just face planted on the pavement. Then dad pulled the car right next to him and told him, "You touch my son again, I'll come find you and your parents and beat you all up." Now this sounds brutal to people nowadays but that is how it was back then. I was beat up by a bunch of my friends' parents just because I was Turkish. Granted there was never a second time because dad would then…But dad became like that because he realised there was no other way unless he became like that. They would have killed me without a second thought. They tried to even stab me once with a compass. What happened was this kid ran up to me and bumped me. Then I felt weird. I looked and I was bleeding. I had to go and take shots for whatever so it wouldn't get infected. From what I heard later, one of the teachers told him to do it. Yeah, good times. But dad made me feel safe because he was always looking after my life.

Then my parents put me into private school because they didn't think I would survive in a public high school. I'm thankful for that, I don't think I would have made it through the public system. Even though it was still pretty racist, pretty shitty. Just richer shittiness. There were a lot of Greek-Cypriots and they were more pompous and arrogant pieces of shit than the ones I met when I was a kid. At least the ones when I was a kid had a certain innocence about them. Like I'd get beat up and the bully would come and apologise. Although I didn't help my case as I always tried to fight the biggest guy there. I got beat up everywhere because I always made myself as if I was tough. I wasn't. But I just wanted to show them that, look man, just because you want to hit me, I'm not gonna sit here and take it. It is what it is. And that English school had the worst of them.

I had friends here and there but no one really close because they were mostly foreigners and always leaving. I was really awkward, and I had extreme social anxiety. I just didn't want to make eye contact with anyone. It was really weird, really awkward. I did terribly academically because I just wanted to go home and play video games where I was safe from those people and their eyes. The times I tried making friends, I was never rewarded. People just didn't want to be friends with me.

I got into a fight once. With this fucker who I won't even give him the privilege of saying his name. He just wouldn't lay off with the Turkish comments. He wasn't even fully Cypriot, just a miserable human being. Privileged prick, got everything given to him and so thinks he is edgy. He would walk behind me, making these comments and calling me a "cunt". He continued for a couple of years. One day, I just snapped. He walked by me and I picked up a tavli and started beating him on the head. The teacher came and separated us. I looked away for one second and he punched me in the eye. But here is the cringiest thing ever. When I had let him go to hit him back, this girl in my class threw some things on top of me, I don't know books, rubbish. And I could see in front of my eyes the whole class sides with him even though they knew very well what he had been doing to me. They stood there chanting, "You crazy!" That was an eye opener. After all that, they would take his side just because he could buy them out…

So, you can imagine the type of guy I was, walking into the Interchurch Youth Club when I was eighteen. Technically, I was over the age limit, but they made an exception. I don't know, I guess they just saw something in me. My friend at the time had dragged me there. He had just returned from one of their annual youth camps.

The first night was really nice. I remember thinking this is surreal, everyone is so nice and welcoming. I mean I didn't really speak to anyone and then when I finally did speak, they were like smiling and replying back. Talking to me. So different. They didn't point fingers, Oh you are this or that. And that changed me, it broke into me. I was brought into a family. I wasn't there for any other reason other than the fact that I enjoyed being there, enjoyed the people. I was fully at home.

I had actually dreamed of being part of a group like that. Two years before Youth Club, I was outside this building with another friend, just hanging. I remember seeing these beautiful girls and this guy and they were like hugging each other. It wasn't like weird or sexual. I felt something watching that. You could really tell they loved each other. I felt very overwhelmed by that. You can't make this shit up. That feeling…Couple of years later, our youth club ended up going to Nicosia to visit their Youth Club, and it turned out that was the Nicosia youth club at the time. Who would have known? They had touched me, I wanted to be a part of something, somewhere filled with love and care. That's what I wished for and I guess God answered my prayers. Those were the best years of my life. I really was surrounded by people who loved me. That was what the youth group used to be all about.

Because you have to understand that, we were a family built out of love for each other. The bond. And that's what I think we lost. Time changed us and we moved on. I left Youth Club and did other things. I don't want to talk about what went on between us because I don't want to hurt people. But I am so grateful for going through those years. They got me to where I am. They taught me confidence, how to love and be loved, and how to not take bullshit from people. Maybe a different way from dad. Maybe it brought me more losses, maybe I became an enemy at the end. Of a different kind. An enemy like for other people. Not because I was part Turkish but I can even take that now. I've learnt that as we grow, we develop, and we become more of who we want to be if we are given the tools to become that person. Who do I want to be? Somebody who can stand up for those I love, win battles not for some glory but because if not, who will? My dad, he saved me and now maybe I can do the same. For my friends, for my family. For love. It is what it is, it is what it is.'

I am CALEB

I left Cyprus even though my heart goes out to this country.

'I remember that was the last prayer that I ever did. I had prayed, "Now is your time, prove to me you are there. That this is all worth something, Please, this is all I am asking. I haven't asked for anything for so long but I am asking for this just…save him, please save him. Save Levi."

I even sent a prayer request out, I was like I need to get back to my religion at this point just in case I was wrong, I didn't want to take chances. I didn't feel like I could take a chance with this thing when it affects someone's life. I sent the prayer request out. I waited. Then someone messaged me back. Instead of condolences or just a, "I am praying for him" etc. they asked me a very damaging question: "Is he saved?"

Because his life wasn't worth the prayer, if his soul didn't belong to them.'

The floor is hard, cold. The minutes passing. The phone screen's lights dimming and then brightening, suddenly, with each new message. Life ticks on, unsympathetic towards the crumbled body in the corner. As if its weight is merely a burden, something to lose, something to ignore, forget. Drink pills and it will disappear within two weeks, the pain turn to numbness, and the dry eyes a habit no longer noticed. A message, the screen lights up again.

There are so many ways to say "sorry". Caleb tries to count all the different variants the congregation has already shared with him. But in the end, they all blend into one. Something like sorry, but something else as well.

It has been a year since Caleb last set foot in Church. Even then, his mind was not committed, doubting. They called him the 'lost sheep' but he never asked for them to shepherd him. Not after all that had happened. But they had ignored that. Were they just waiting for him to fall? How many of them when the prayer request had come through, were gloating? Nodding to themselves in an 'I told you so' attitude, that yes this was God's work against their fallen brother, his judgement against the accused, and his getting Caleb back to where he belonged. Back to Church. Back to them.

'Of course Levi wasn't saved. He wasn't a Christian. I remember actually throwing the phone across the wall, breaking the phone. I was so annoyed. It was just such a conflict of emotions. Death was not something I could easily deal with. It took at least three or four years for me to cry about my dad's death. I take it really hard. That for me just felt like there was something flawed in this system, this Church. And to this day I still feel it is a flawed judicial system. It does not work. It is not comprehensible to me that you can have someone as evil as Hitler and then he says sorry and then he is fine. And then someone who leads a good life and do all the good that he can and just because he didn't have evidence to support that belief, he ends up burning in hell for eternity. It was that flaw in the judicial system that was the catalyst for me to break away completely.'

They had been his family, his church family. There was that time Caleb remembered drawing-up a family tree featuring his friends at Youth Club. They all became mothers, fathers, sisters or brothers, even grandmothers and grandfathers. All fake, of course, but it never felt so. There had been something there. Those smiles in the Facebook photos of old Youth Club camps and events. *They must have meant something*. It had meant something to all of them being there. They all wanted it, they all chose to turn up. *How did it all go so wrong?*

'I was born in Cyprus. My mum is fully Cypriot but my mum had been brought up in London and my dad was from Manchester. At the age of three, I was diagnosed with acute lymphoblastic leukemia. The next few years were tough. I had to go through intense chemotherapy treatments. But it wasn't only the physical side that was exhausting and difficult. It was watching children beside me who I would later learn died from the same diagnosis I had. There were children that were dying in the early 90s all the time. There wasn't a high survival rate. I was one of the lucky ones. I survived.

I have so many memories of that time, that period really impacted my life. I remember, I was always hugging the nurses. They adored me, I think they really loved me. I really loved them back. I tried to marry them all. I was quite a little flirt as a four year old. I never had the time to properly learn Greek between treatments. I only learnt English. English was more of my mum's native tongue and for my dad as well. That was a struggle. It also set me a bit back with my schooling in Cyprus till my treatment was complete. I started public school late and I had to do my first grade and my second grade in the first year.

So, my mum's idea was, Oh, he will learn the language (Greek), let me just throw him in there. That was really frustrating for me. I have a distinct memory of being in class and wanting a specific color pencil from the other side of the room but not finding the words to say it in Greek. I just started crying and pointing towards it. I was already a sensitive child and I don't know if that contributed to my sensitivity at all though I think it did quite a lot. I felt really out of place there and was made to feel it. Throughout the next years I was the target of ongoing bullying. Not physical but there was a lot of name-calling, a lot of picking on. I was called 'Englezoui', the English kid, because English was more of my first language. They would grab my school bag and throw it out and stuff like that. I never blended in and that was also because I was, you know, quite a gay child. I don't know in terms of how that was interpreted by others but I felt it internally that I wasn't quite the heteronorm. Kids were absolutely cruel about those things.

I had one friend during my time in primary school. He was English and he was my best friend because we could talk in English. And then I would also hang around with girls and stuff. I did have a child psychologist in the school commenting on my choice of friends, asking, "Why do you hang out with girls? You should hang out more with the boys." Even at that age, they were trying to impose something on me.

My mother knew I was being bullied constantly and she tried to protect me from it by putting me into private school after I graduated from primary school, which I was really thankful for. Even though it didn't really get better in private schools either. You just get richer shittier kids, little brats. And there I was, we weren't really rich, we didn't have a lot growing-up so I had more of the second-hand clothes from my cousins and stuff like that. While the kids in my class would have new shoes and this and that every week. Again, I felt out of place but I was so used to it at that point, it didn't affect me as much. The good thing was that it was such a lift off of my shoulders when I could just speak in English and comfortably communicate. I loved communicating with people so having those language barriers at the public school was so frustrating to me. I was around thirteen when I started private school. I hadn't seen my dad since I was seven at this point, he had remained in Manchester. We weren't talking, and maybe my mum wanted it to be that way, an escape... Their marriage did not turn out as it could have been. But at thirteen, we got a knock on the door and it was a family friend I had never seen before. She informed my mum that my dad had recently passed away. I didn't actually have a massive reaction because I was still so angry. I was a very angry kid. I didn't really know how to react, I never learnt how to react to death. It only hit me much much later. But I remember at that moment feeling a bit shocked at how upset my mum was. "Oh, I didn't think you liked him" was my comment, I believe. I had a lot of defences up and it took actually a few years after that to feel the mental impact of his passing.

I think about my dad these days, I think about him all the time. I really wish he can be around. I imagine what our chats could have been like now. Because when you are a child you can never really fully communicate. It is different talking as adults. Just seeing a parent be proud of how you grow, and what you have done in life. It is kind of that I really miss. But life is life.

By fourteen I had a very close friend in high school. She was quite a rebel and different and we were the outcasts of the class. We were just different and we didn't give a shit about it. Playing video games, really into anime. I was literally at her house all the time and I became very close with the whole family. They became my family, too. One day, my friend's mother, who was a Christian, took us to a youth club. I had no clue what it was, I was only fourteen. I didn't know it was actually religious. I don't come from a religious background. My mum is quite an agnostic, she will light a candle in the church and do her prayers by herself but was never really vocal about her beliefs. And she never tried to force any kind of ideology on me. She was very nice in that aspect.

But this was a Christian gathering and the religious aspect was never hidden. It was an outreach project towards teenagers in the local community, run in English. Youth Club evenings had a pattern to them. We would play games, hang out, sing some worship songs and have a short talk on a theme or subject based on the Bible. It seemed quite harmless at the time. What my friend and I were really loving was hanging out because we were so ostracised in our class and we didn't get along with that typical chav, brav person in school. These people were different and they seemed far more accepting. It just made us feel so much more comfortable. Because, hey in this environment, I didn't think people would want to attack me. In school, you just walk down the corridor and anything can be off. You wear something that you think is cool and some kid teases you, and it completely destroys your day or month. In this environment, it was very different. We became a family, it really felt like that.

The issue though that I began seeing was the points of infiltration of the youth leaders, asking me, getting to know my life, prodding to find what was missing. And they really anchored onto my dad being gone. I remember one youth leader saying, "You might have lost your Earth father but you have an Eternal Father." They made this my life, they tied me to that statement. This was the beginning, and as an emotionally sensitive teenager who was already struggling with anger, it just added up to the conflicts within me regarding my sexuality and my race (I have Afro-Caribbean roots as well). I don't think I was ever really vocal about these roots. I mean, everybody could guess I had some black heritage. For instance, they would ask about my lips. I remember my mum once looking at me and saying, "You keep pursing your lips." Because I kept doing that subconsciously, I didn't want to stand out, I wanted to fit in. That meant, I thought, having thinner lips. That was a point at which people could look at and think, "Oh, you are not fully Cypriot, are you?" Or something like that. I was really struggling to find my place. There at Youth Club they sell you this idea that it doesn't matter, you will fit in. Which is a beautiful message, I don't disagree. But what flows in after is when it starts getting murky. You start going into dark waters.

I was very into it though, I was quite dedicated. I spent many years there, moving up the ranks, becoming a youth leader at some point later on. I got to know the inner workings behind it all, the recruitment, the selling points. I bought into it all and so did so many others. I am a very mechanical thinker in terms of I have a book and I have a bunch of rules and I think we should follow all these rules. In that respect, I was their perfect candidate, I guess. I was the person in that group that convinced everyone that pirating materials is theft. Something that really stuck on me. No, but it is logical, because it says here in this part of the book that it is stealing and if we are breaking pirating rules that is classified as stealing. And we need to follow the rules of the government still. I followed all the rules to the last letter.

Of course, my homosexual tendencies needed to be suppressed, I didn't even need to tell the youth leader about them. I knew what they would say to me, and I was doing all the work myself on myself so what was the point of telling anybody anyway? I knew the rules, I already knew it was bad and so it was in the form of denying myself that I thought I could kind of get over it. "Through the power of God, dadadadada. I will overcome it." I would feel the attraction, I recognized it but I never acted upon it. At one point, I even became homophobic, hating what was inside of me, and hating myself because of their and my hate. To be a part of them, you needed to share that hatred, and not just share but be violently committed to it.'

'University was probably the biggest breaking point. Now I was no longer surrounded by my clique from Youth Club, where everyone had the same opinion as me and we just patted each other on the back with, "Yes yes yes, that is correct." You are kind of each confirming your own beliefs. It is such a comfort zone. The new territory finally put me in a situation where I was surrounded by people who were not of the same ideology or faith as me. On the one hand, I had the attitude that I was going to

evangelise, that it was a great opportunity, but of course you go there and you realise it is not as easy as you thought. I think the most powerful impact on me at that stage was seeing just the good in people who didn't necessarily share my belief.

I remember one situation with a friend of mine who is actually now an atheist. I remember we were at a hospital, actually, picking up another friend to take her home and we were waiting outside of the ward. There was this little old lady in a wheelchair and these people were like trying to get her into the car. He, the friend with me, just kind of ran to help them to get her in. And I remember seeing that and thinking, I wonder why he did that. If a Christian were to do that, they would do it to prove something to their God. Is that sincere or is it to win points? I began to really contemplate things, and I looked into my own sexuality at that point. I was like twenty and I was not sure how convinced I was with any of that anymore. I remember calling Youth Club and asking for a break from my duties as youth leader. Then, for a period of time, I felt far more open, far more comfortable. I mean, with the gay thing, I was still very very shy. The max thing I did was kiss a guy. And that was as far as I would take it. It was still something I was battling with. The breaking point was Levi and my last prayer, my prayer for Levi. It was after that where the real journey began.'

I stepped away. I needed some time away from the island, so I did an Erasmus to a different country. The chains were lifted and I saw a different side of society. I saw that people can be happy without that strict ideology. I was able to experiment. Become myself because there no one knew me. No one could control me. I was out of reach completely. And it was as soon as I returned that I came out. I was ready to.

Coming out was exhausting. Every time it felt like such a, "I need to talk to you about something and it is serious." Well, I wouldn't say it is serious but people's reactions would make it seem so serious. I even had people tell me, "Why didn't you tell me before?" and make it about themselves. I was like, "Hold on, this is about me right now, this is my moment. I am sharing something that is very personal. I had to come to a conclusion, I had to be comfortable with myself, with my own identity before coming out to everyone else." I remember having one discussion with someone from the Youth Club to whom I came out to. We went out for a coffee. We were still close at that point, well, until that discussion. We were sitting, talking and I kind of wanted to come out to her because she was my friend. I told her and she was like OK, you know, and we began discussing it. In a nutshell, she basically paralleled my sexuality to an eating disorder. A mental disorder that I needed to "fix". That I was sick because I was attracted to men rather than women. Back fifty years into the past. That for me was like, why am I sitting and taking this shit from these people. What the hell? I was just astounded.

She was the turning point. She became the exception to my own rule. I am so open to people discussing my sexuality but not her, not after that. And she still believes it. After all these years, some of them still believe in that tale. They were my friends... And that for me was confirmation that there was and is something sinister going on at least around here in this Christian community. It did not feel right. I don't know what happened but maybe it is because they stopped questioning themselves, others, not out of maliciousness but out of sheer curiosity. Maybe they are too scared to find themselves wrong, maybe they are too scared to find themselves at all.

I left Cyprus even though my heart goes out to this country. I truly believe it is a beautiful place. But right now there is no place for me here. As I am now and who I have become, Cyprus is not ready for me. Nor am I ready to face what it was and what it has become.'

At times, a prayer request will go out to all the members

of the Church. A name and a short sentence, a plea for help or encouragement, an answer for the heart. Maybe some are answered, some left unread, deleted. Texts, emails, Caleb no longer receives any from the Church. He had removed himself from the prayer chain a good while back. Just after Levi passed away, just after the last drop of faith fell like a tear across a cheek, down a trail across Caleb's skin, past gritted teeth, and then free falling onto that cold cold floor. *Save Levi*, there was no more saving to do. It was too late for that. Though in a play of words, in its own small happenings and strange occurrences, Levi saved. Levi saved Caleb.

I am LUSINE

Even though I have never been to Armenia, I feel very Armenian.

'As a child I grew up in the Piraeus area of Athens, where the port is. It's a place where there used to be lots of immigrants and Greeks that used to come from areas occupied by Turks like Constantinople and Polis, these areas. We grew up in a very family-like neighbourhood, if I may say that. My parents had brothers and sisters living there so I had many cousins. I grew up in Greece but we were Armenian. But we only spoke Armenian at home. We had all the Armenian traditions and we celebrated Christmas on the sixth of January, which is usually the twenty-fifth in Greek Orthodox tradition. I went to an Armenian primary school and our family ran a Lebanese-Armenian restaurant because my parents were immigrants from Lebanon to Greece during the war in Lebanon (1975-1990). I grew up in that, in food and everything. I was in a very protective environment.

The restaurant was popular at its time. I remember it was the first one in Greece. That is what I remember as a kid, that we used to have lots of actors because actors always like to try new things. So, we used to have known people come. And people would have to travel to come because Piraeus is far from other parts of Greece. They would come a long way to come. I was serving as a kid and I used to get lots of tips because I was like a little girl. I grew up in the restaurant, which has also helped with my character being more social, sleeping with any loud noise, loud music. I did love it.

But there were only Armenian primary schools in Greece. We didn't have any secondary schools. There was one just a gymnasium and that didn't really encourage (even though it was Armenian) the Armenian culture and society. My parents decided to send me to Cyprus, which is a school that is (even though all Armenian) very multicultural because all the Armenians are from around the world. It continued my Armenian culture and origin.'

Cyprus has been a home to Armenian nationals since the sixth century. After the death of Leo VI, the last king of Armenia, leadership was inherited by his cousin, James I de Lusignan, who, at that time, was also the king of Cyprus. At his appointment, he became the king of Armenia, Cyprus and Jerusalem. Later, Cyprus served as a centre of refuge for the victims of the Ottoman's genocide of Armenians, known as the Armenian Holocaust, during the early twentieth century. In its aftermath, brothers Krikor and Garabed Melkonian founded an orphanage in Cyprus' capital city, Nicosia, for the forsaken children of Armenian descent in Anatolia. The institute became known as the Melkonian Educational Institute. Later, the school also acted as an accredited boarding school for the children of the Armenian diaspora worldwide. With so many children being raised in Cyprus through this school's system, the Armenian community in Cyprus grew rapidly. In the 1960 constitution, the Armenians were among the three religious communities to be officially recognised by the Cypriot state, along with the Latins (Roman Catholics) and the Maronites. Today, the Armenian diaspora is spread across the world with a significant community on the island, many of whom are Melkonian graduates.

'My sisters had come here before me to the school. I knew, even when I was small, that when the time came, I would also come here. When I was 11, I packed my luggage and with the group, escorted by adults, I came to Cyprus. Not my parents, maybe one adult for the whole group.

There were kids from all over the world at the school. It was small, only 250 but I had friends from Romania, Albania, Bulgaria, USA, United Kingdom, Turkey. Now, I have friends everywhere. You learn things about everyone and everywhere.'

The forest of trees that stand as a protective wall before the school was planted by the first orphans residing on campus. Each tree serves as a living monument for all the lives lost during the Genocide, its branches constantly reaching to the heavens in prayers for the souls of ancestors past, and descendants present.

'It was a very closed environment. People wouldn't be allowed to come in and we didn't have much time to go out. I had a few friends from outside but they were also Armenians. I got to know them through friends that were Armenians in Cyprus that wouldn't stay over in the school but attended day classes. When sometimes we would go over to their house and their friends would be there, that is how we met. But we didn't have any other like just Cypriot friends.

But we had ourselves. We used to sleep with our friends. We would do after school activities together and we would go out once a month, when we were in the second and third grade, which was the first three years of school, and then it would be two times a month and then as you got older every weekend. And we used to walk Limassol Avenue until Ledra. We had a completely different relationship than just classmates. We were so close.

The teachers used to have a building behind our place. But only for those who used to come from abroad because we would have teachers coming specifically for the school from England because it was an English-based curriculum on O-Level and A-Level. We would spend a lot of time together with our teachers. I loved going back to Greece for a holiday for a week or so and then I just missed Cyprus again. Like I work at a school now and I work with a few of my ex-teachers. They always say, even now, that the bond we used to have with the students in that school, they have never experienced again even though they have worked in other schools because there your parents were not around. You would always look up to your teachers, get advice from them and see them as your parents sometimes as well.

I was the last year that went to school and graduated in 2004. And it was the last year that it worked as a school and then it closed down. And the next year it was just that class that was going to graduate and they arranged for everyone to go to other schools so now it is closed and it is sad. It was the reason I fell in love with Cyprus.

Before I was going to graduate, in my last year I was telling my dad I would really like to stay in Cyprus and study there. And he was like, "No, you have to come here". We would argue. We had a shop then, we had closed down the restaurant and had a shop so he wanted me also to help with the family business and study in Greece and be there. He wouldn't agree with me staying in Cyprus. And I did go to Greece and I did sit the exams of the Greek university and I just decided I couldn't take Greece any more and so I left everything and I came on my own to Cyprus.

I had a boyfriend at the time and I stayed with him. He was not Armenian but Cypriot. And I had met him through my sister who was living here but my dad told me he was never talking to me again because I had left and I went against his will. Because my dad was one of those who they say what happened to you, and they decided your life for you even when you were 30. I had some support because I had somebody here and his family was supportive. But when I came to Cyprus, I didn't know what to study. The colleges at that time were just colleges, they weren't even universities like they are now. Their courses were not accredited, and I didn't know what to do. For a few months, I worked until I could see what I was going to do, and then I decided to study to be a beautician. I never even used to apply make-up before because I didn't know how it was done. But it was the only accredited thing and because I was so much into science and biology and chemistry and beautician did a lot of courses on anatomy and physiology. I said, "Ok, I'll try it", so I did go and studied between working full-time and I enjoyed it in the end.

My classmates were mostly Cypriot girls. They had no idea how the world was. They were still living with their parents and they were overpampered, which I wasn't used to. I had been eleven when I had to fix my own bed, do my own laundry, clean my own room, be responsible for studying, be responsible for shopping and managing my finances whatever my parents would send me. But they liked me because I really helped them with anatomy and physiology, which they were clueless about. They wouldn't see me as Armenian, they would see me as Greek from Greece. I didn't feel any racism or discrimination. I always introduced myself as Armenian from Greece. I told them that I grew up in Greece and was raised in Greece but I was Armenian because that is how I felt as well. I still feel Armenian even though I have never been to Armenia, I feel very Armenian. And that is because of my dad and how he managed to always put that in us.

He died recently. Just after my son was born. He taught me to love my Armenian heritage, he really set that up. Now I am raising my son and I really wish he could experience what I experienced at the Melkonian School. It really made me who I am today. My dad began it but the school built the Armenian heritage inside me, inside all of us at that school.'

What would she see walking through the gates of the Melkonian Institute today. The forest thick with its own dark evergreens, the fallen needles of the cypress trees lined up in rows of, of…observance, defence, rest? Would she stare at the walls of the main building, the faded mustard yellow, feel their roughness with the back of her hand, wonder who or what sits behind the drawn curtains covering the long, barred windows? Feel the eerie quietness of the courtyard despite its being set not far from one of the busiest roads of Nicosia, a disquietness of walking alone across the gravel yard towards the monuments at the back. Past the basketball courts with no baskets, the boarding quarters with no boarders, the emptiness of it all other than the occasional crow landing atop an arch, a karkaaaar screeched against the stranger, the lone walker making her way through the mud and puddles on that dreary January day. A shadow at the mausoleum of the Melkonian Brothers. Footsteps remembering the spots where they used to stand or sit around with friends during break time, talk of teacher this and teacher that, their crushes and their worries, their hopes and dreams for the future. Fingers tracing letters by the soil of the trees, inscribing themselves into the roots. *Home.* And again. *Home.*

Cat & Mouse

I am AUDREY

"This is Cyprus".
It's the explanation for everything.

There is no 'I' in 'we'. But there is an 'I' in family. There is no I in 'belong' but there is an 'I' in 'belonging'. Maybe the 'I' feels so alone at times because it only comes later, only after belong has made its mark and is ready to reach out. An invitation. Belonging comes after belong and it can be such a long drawn out road. Alone and lonely. But is loneliness belonging?

'I'm from the U.S. I moved to Germany when I was around twenty to be a Nanny for one or two years. I stayed there for seventeen years because I married a German. I never liked living in the US anyway. As soon as I got the chance, I travelled. I went to Japan for a month when I was fifteen as part of an exchange program and absolutely loved it. I went to Costa Rica when I was seventeen for seven weeks and then to Mexico for a year when I was eighteen. Finally, to Germany. I was only going to do one year of the apprenticeship and then quit. Then my husband, well he wasn't my husband just yet, showed up with roses and the rest is history.

My husband wanted to leave Germany from as far back as I can remember. I mean from the very first time I met him, he was talking about doing an exchange to the Philippines, I think. I teased him that he only married an American in the hopes of leaving Germany but we ended up having to live there for another fifteen years. But he wanted to go full time into mission work. We had finished a course with a disciple school and there were so many opportunities. He was offered a place in administration in Montana in the US, but he didn't really want to do that. There was an opportunity to work with a children's home in Thailand. We prayed about it and felt it was a no. We had an opportunity to go to Peru, although the family was not too excited, prayed about it and again a no. But we kept trying to leave Germany.

Cyprus was looking to find people to help found a House of Prayer and my husband was looking for someplace, anywhere in the world, where he could get involved full-time with intercessory prayer. Finally, the answer to our prayers was a yes.'

Audrey's daughter flicks through a book of fairytales. It is the *Ugly Duckling*. She reads out a sentence, a moment caught out of context. At one point she laughs at a picture that had been colored over by another 'reader', grey and blue breaking the fixed outlines of the duckling. A reader who may well be an early revolutionary or an eager admirer of expressionism.

"Mummy, look how someone is trying to paint the ugly ducklings."

"Baby swans. An ugly duckling is not actually a duck. It's a swan. It never was a duck. A swan just doesn't make a good duck."

"It's grey."

"Yes, it is grey. Baby swans are grey. Cygnets. Baby swans are called cygnets."

Her daughter returns to her musing. With her small fingers, she points to words and pictures, allowing them to create a tale she can believe in. Of swans in familiar ponds, of swans in foreign ponds. Soon the book will be abandoned on her seat, when her attention is taken up with something else. Breakfast. As the dark eyes of the cygnet stares out of the book, no one pays it any more attention.

'At the beginning, I did feel really isolated because I had five children, my husband was busy all the time and I was just sitting in the house. I really wanted to learn Greek. I started going to the Greek Tots meetings but there were very few native speakers of Greek there. We were all there to learn. There was one Cypriot lady who would come in for the last half hour and do songs for the children. But, then again, I learnt more at Greek Tots from that half hour singing at the end in Greek than I did from three years of government classes. There I had three different teachers, three different books, three different styles. I mean the teacher was giving us the answers for the final exam and that bothered me. I have a lovely certificate that says I speak Greek to the Level of B1. Yeah right.

We had mice at home and, when I realised we had mice, I wanted a trap that would kill them. Yes, I know, I am horrible. And I went to this one store that they speak good English but they didn't have the kind of trap I wanted. I knew exactly what I wanted. We had bought the same trap in Germany. I did not want the wooden one with the wire where you see the whole dead mouse's body and everything. But I did want the mouse dead. So, I went to this other place and there were two people there. Neither of them spoke any English so they didn't understand when I said I wanted a "mousetrap". Instead I had to think outside the box. I said, "Exo ena… Oxi. Exo pontikaki. Pontikakia. Den thelo Pontikakia. Thelo bam." It worked! I had 'pontikaki' from this song we were doing at Tots. I didn't know if I was saying 'mousey' or if I was saying some cute little baby word, or if it was a real word. They laughed but they showed me their mouse traps. I got the exact mousetrap that I wanted. Same brand that I had in Germany. It closes on the mouse's head so you don't see the mouse's head. Then you pick up the trap, hold it over the bin and out it goes. Now we have cats to do the job.

A conversation I've had like, I'm very capable of exaggerating but I'm possibly not exaggerating when I say possibly dozens of times, is when someone says to me, "Why you no speak Greek? You live in Cyprus! You must speak Greek!" and then I answer in Greek, "Thelo na matho Ellinika".

"Yes, that's because you no speak Greek!"

"Why are you speaking in English with me?"

"Because you no speak Greek!"

"But I'm trying to speak Greek with you! Mprospatho!"

This has been my life for nine years here in Cyprus. People make it very difficult to learn Greek.'

The thing about the Ugly Duckling is that it had the choice. To stay or leave, to pretend that whatever it was hearing around itself was but a confirmation of its existence, and to persevere, as if through the shivers against those cold winter nights, the inability to communicate with the old woman or the children from the farmyard, there could be nothing but the warmth of hope that one day the sun will come out and the others return. The choice to see the snow melt away and be ready rather than melt away with the slow retreat of the season. To be lonely with the knowledge that with the blooming of spring, the loneliness will disappear, like a bad dream. With that, belonging will be merely a winter's tale, a cold dream. Sometimes, even choosing is a dream.

'You've heard the phrase, "This is Cyprus". It's the explanation for everything. You're not allowed to get upset and you can't do anything about it. Mostly I'm OK with that but sometimes it's annoying. I had a car accident recently. I was coming out of the supermarket parking lot and I wanted to turn right but because cars are parked illegally 100% of the time and it's hard to see around the corner. I nosed the car out a bit more and one car flew

out on the street at a lot more than the legal 50 kmph and I had to slam on my breaks. I was a little shaky by that and either I didn't look very well or that car was going faster than I thought. So, we hit each other as I came out. I didn't even feel the crash. I heard the crunch so I stopped. His entire side of the car, all the way from the front bumper to the back bumper was dented and scratched. It had rubbed off most of my number plate.

He stopped another fifteen meters on but he wasn't pushed that way at all. Obviously, I stopped quickly and he went, "Chouuuuum". I got out of the car and I realised I just hit my next door neighbour. We both got out of our cars. First of all it was like, "Hi! What happened?" He wasn't yelling at me or anything. We called the insurance people and I told my neighbor we should move the cars. He said we should wait for the insurance to come first. I said, "It was my fault. I'm not going to try and say that it wasn't. You know where I live. Let's just move the cars to the side. We don't need to call the police. Nobody is hurt."

In Cyprus even though it's a teeny tiny fender bender, you're supposed to leave the cars exactly where they are. That's because part of the mentality is that you argue that you are right and the other was wrong no matter what. It's tradition. That was a little confusing for him that I said it was my fault because whether he had been going too fast or not, was not the question or whether someone was parked illegally was not the question. He was on the road and had right of way and I was coming out. So, therefore, it was my fault. To me that was very clear. Also, this is Cyprus. He is Cypriot and I'm not, I didn't have a chance. He's male, I'm female, I didn't have a chance. He's eighty-two years old and I'm not a spring chicken at forty-seven, but I didn't have a chance. I saw no point in arguing. While waiting for the insurance guy, so many people who were shopping came to say, "Hi, oh hello, how are you? What happened?" and then I assure you the entire neighbourhood knew within a few minutes because this is

Cyprus. They all knew. They're nice here. One guy I knew rode past on his motorcycle and waved hello. I waved back. And with that I'm just accepting this culture.

In the States, I never felt that I fit in and here I don't fit in either, but no one expects me to. In the States, I always felt like the ugly duckling. "You don't belong here. You're not part of us. We're not the same so we want nothing to do with you." Here they look at me and say, "Well, that's odd but you're American and you can't help it." They will still interact with me if that makes sense. They don't expect me to blend in, I can just be me. And somehow I belong and it is not so lonely.'

I am MATEO

All blending together on that stage, there in Cyprus, coming together for Cyprus.

He sits upon the step, strumming his ukulele. His long hair is wild in the breeze, with that one dreadlock, thin, hardly twitching as it stretches over his left shoulder. An elderly couple walks by each wearing matching 'I love Cyprus' caps and baggy knee length khakis. Then another, younger, whispering to each other in what may be Swedish, or German. Next come the locals, families of pulling children, mothers with bright lipstick and brighter heels, and maybe a father, dressed down, clutching his phone like he would the hand of his child, but it isn't. Two young women walk past, one blonde, the other dark, holding hands and exchanging blushes. A group of five or six men, just finished from the day's construction work, chalk and dirt still clinging to their arms, cheeks and hair. The colour of their trousers is hard to make out after the last three month's work. One, with narrow eyes, and skin the colour of tamarind, glances at the boy but does not make a move to stop and listen. Instead, he draws out the remainder of the lunch his boss had provided that day, sandwiches, and chews on the bread. Slowly, the crowd thins. A few women holding hands with what appears to be their boss' children, continue shaking their heads, repeating 'nao, nao, nao' persistently, but drowsily, as if getting the child home is one step closer to their own bed, just one more step…

And then the street is empty and in that emptiness the

sweet vibrations of the strings, as if in meditation echo against the shop walls. He himself sits with his eyes closed, a soft smile on his lips, and his thin body breathing in and out, in and out with the plucking of strings, against a quietness of a by-street near Ledra. Out of the corner, where a pile of pack-up boxes has been dumped from the nearby outlet store, a tabby cat tentatively walks out. Its ears are poised towards the instrument, towards the mysterious boy charming its senses with music. One step, pause, two steps, pause again, and when no danger appears, another step and another. Then, without a pause, it leaps into the boy's lap and curls up, its purr vibrating louder and louder. The boy is a young man really, the cat must have noticed the black beard growing along the chin. But there was no fear as it settled for a long slumber against the thighs of the musician. He, Mateo, opens his eyes at the feeling of something soft pressing against his legs and smiles as the cat merely stares back at him, no inclination of leaving its comfortable spot. As if they have known each other for a long time. *Pied Piper of Cats*, he thinks to himself, before closing his eyes again and settling into a new rhythm.

'I am from South America but I was adopted at three months old and moved to the United States. I lived in Rhode Island, then my parents got divorced and I moved to Chicago with my mum. My dad left to go to Cyprus. He moved to Cyprus because it was always a dream of his even as a kid in Rhode Island, when my parents were still married. That he would open up a practice in Greece or Cyprus. My father is a neurosurgeon. My entire family are neurosurgeons and doctors and rocket scientists. It's nuts. And my uncle is Greek so his family is in Athens. They, my father and uncle, have been business partners since they were much much younger, like he was a student of my father's.

At fifteen, my grades were kind of shit, and my mum was using it as a ploy.

"If you don't shape up, I'll send you to go live with your father in Cyprus."

But by the end of the year, I had so much happen in that one year, like I had four of my friends die in that year, I had a bunch of family problems, I was going through my own struggles, personally, and at the end of the year, my grades were fine, like all As and Bs and two C's. I mean I had never worked well with the American education system whatever it was at that point. I have ADHD and I used to skip a lot of school. And I hadn't lived with my father since I was eight. I was like hey, nothing is keeping me here in Chicago, all this craziness is happening, change would be good and it is probably the best decision I have ever made in my entire life.

Especially before fucking Donald Trump, fuck Donald Trump seriously, I am blessed to not live in that country any more. But I still have the citizenship, which sucks, what with being American in the Middle East. Having people have these concepts of what an American is, having never come across an American and just seeing what an American does (Trump). Living here in Cyprus you might get people who won't treat you the same just because you are an American living in this part of the world. They see what an American does in the media and they think you are the same. I don't have the same views as the majority of those American people but I am still connected to them. And that is some stuff I got into deep confrontations with my mother about, what you, as an American abroad, have to deal with. I am living a boat ride away from war. Yet, you are here in the West cozy, debating whether Donald Trump should stop tweeting, or whether he should tweet more, like this is benign bullshit. The world is in chaos and there are people dying in

Africa, in Europe, in the Middle East, there is shit happening everywhere, it is not centralised it is everywhere. But the West always sees it specific to one thing, always trying to find a fucking scapegoat. But there isn't one answer to everything because it is everywhere. But I am American.

For the things that the American government has done, I have to apologise. Oh, fuck yeah, I had to apologise a bunch of times and to many many different types of people for the shit that my government was doing. Like in the past two years I have thought about ripping up my passport countless times. Because if I was going to be drafted, fuck that. I am no longer an American citizen the second World War Three breaks out, I am not fighting for a country I don't believe in, I am not fighting for no country. If I am here, I'd better keep this place safe. I can't put everything aside just because a piece of paper says I have to. Like, unfortunately, that is what I will do. I will destroy my fucking passport. I have apologised many many times for the shit that the government has done. And, of course, it is uncomfortable but at the same time I want people to know that, especially people who in this part of the world don't come across Americans terribly often, and all they see is what they see on TV, I want them to know we are not all like that. Within the sense of this, I just want people to realise we are not all the same. We are not all like that, we don't all believe that. It is hard but I want it to be done, I want people to feel comfortable. Just like I, wherever I go, I want to feel comfortable, safe and content so I try to do the best for anybody that I come across as well.

So, I moved to Cyprus. Went to an international school. When I first came in and still didn't have a grasp of the language, I definitely felt like an outsider. I never conform to anyone's group, or parea, I have always just been myself. It was much easier to feel like an outsider when I first got here. Once I learnt the language, it kind of opened up a bit more and they would feel a little more comfortable because I was able to speak back and forth with them. Because I would respond in English and they would understand yet they were still able to speak to me in Greek. So, it kind of made more comfortable communication.

I have been playing music my entire life. Music is all I do and it is all I have ever done. Even when I was a baby, two or three years old, my parents tell me this but I also remember this, taking pots and pans out of the cupboards and tapping on them for hours, hours hours hours hours. Hours and hours and hours. I play saxophone, ukulele and anything percussion. But if I was able to learn something classically in school, I would have gone into that afterwards. But before I could finish high school in Cyprus, my dad moved me to Athens. Some friends of mine were just starting a band here in Cyprus and they needed a percussionist, which sucked because I was then living in Athens. So, I introduced the lead singer to one of my friends from my school days in the South who played the percussion. But afterwards, once I finished high school, I was thinking, what do I want to do with my life. Cyprus was the only place I wanted to go, so I moved back here.

Whilst I was still in Athens, the band had started to make their music with some gigs here and there. When I moved back, they already had kind of a name for themselves, and I was just inducted into the band. And, eventually, my friend who was doing the percussion left, and I became the only percussionist. We started touring North and South, gigs on both sides. We actually played more on the North those few years than we had on the South. People there dance more, they are more open to being free like that. On the South, people don't move around as much. We didn't really know what our genre was reggae fusion kind of, it is kind of like a peace love unity type of music, just a fusion of a bunch of different things. We had ukulele, acoustic guitar, electric base, then I played a cajón, that box drum, djembe that Afri-

can drum and the toumberleki, the Greek or Turkish hand drum. Our band actually more or less, at least on the North, was like the only band that had the majority of their set be original stuff. So, that also made us stand out. We were mostly made-up of immigrants, non-Cypriots. I don't think you will ever be able to get that anywhere else in the world. Like five people in the band and they are all from different countries. Columbian but raised in the States, Filipino, Belarussian-Cypriot, full Cypriot and then Finnish. And when we played, every instrument usually seemed to be playing something completely different but everything ends up meshing together perfectly, that was us. All blending together on that stage, there in Cyprus, coming together for Cyprus.

Our lyrics were directed towards our experience living there on the island. And the divide that this country was going through. It influenced our music in a very big way. We sang about the political climate in Cyprus, the "Cyprus Problem". I think it just happens when you live in this country long enough. Even for two years, it doesn't need to be longer than that. You become part of the politics just by living in the city and whether or not you want, are passionate about it or maybe you will just ignore it. The people I surrounded myself with always tended to maintain a passion for peace, I guess. And people's reactions to our songs were always positive, it made them think, it made them talk about it.

Like one song from our album, it is called "Patience". It is one of the slower ones. Some of them are really slow, some of them are more upbeat, some of them are really intense, fun dancing-around instrumental parts but this is one of the really chill ones. It is about eight minutes long. When I first heard it after it was mastered, I thought back on the moment, like the foray you feel when you just find that pocket with a bunch of other people around you, the build we had as well, our music is the little things, that building. Building something there and build-

ing something with our music. Even if it just builds conversation. The lyrics, that is what they do and the music that is what it does. Because we are all…

"Waiting for the hopes of tomorrow,
Waiting for the shadows of solitude
To pass, to pass…"[1]

It is getting darker now, cooler. People resume their walk back and forth along the street. Faces turn towards the young man, playing slower now, softer, as if in contemplation, as if overcome with a strong deep emotion. Something has changed in the vibrations of the string and the cat awakes. It looks up into the creased eyes and Mateo too peers down. In that moment something clicks within the creature and it hops out back onto the street, back towards the old boxes in the corner. But just before it disappears into the shadows, it glances back at Mateo, for just a moment, and in that moment, even in that street of busy legs rushing back and forth, even with voices filling the air, a wave consuming the pitch of the ukulele, Mateo feels something. Connection of a sort. He feels less alone in that world of passer-bys by staring into the eyes of the cat.

---

1 Alex & the Dukes, 'Patience: Demo Version' (October 2016), <https://www.youtube.com/watch?v=sS-pEcgoEkE>

I am JULIEN

'"You are not Cypriot." But I tell them I am. Cyprus is all I have ever known.

'"You are not Cypriot." But I tell them I am. Cyprus is all I have ever known.

"But it's not on your papers." And it goes like that. I've never been to Greece and I've barely been to Lebanon. I grew up here, my whole life has been here. Time and time again, same shit. But I don't care what they say, I am Cypriot.

If I'm not Cypriot, then what am I? There's nothing else. But for some, people can only exist on paper. They can only make sense with what the paper says. So, I'm gonna get that fucking paper and throw it in their faces. Just to say, "Fuck you!" There.'

He's not angry. He is what comes after, that word that combines frustration whilst maintaining patience, sarcasm whilst clinging to an all-time sincere solemnity, laughter whilst taking a drag from a rolled up joint because it isn't a reaction to humour but an attempt to breathe. Maybe he was angry, all those years back, swinging a skinny knuckle and swearing at some kid to go to places that boy did not understand, (he did later, what with French classes at school and Google Translate but that's a different story). That kid, who also ran a gang around Julien's neighbourhood, let go of the canister of petrol he'd been pouring over the body hanging from the banister. Not from fear but to show that 'poushti xeno', that foreign kid, to mind his own business (and a few other things). The body, thrashing, wet with petrol, screeched, its eyes wide, wild. It shook with what little strength it had left, whilst the metal chain at every jerk wrapped tighter around its neck, slitting skin, suffocating its three month throat. It tossed its body forward and back as the body of young Julien was also tossed, forward and back, kicked, punched, jabbed, kicked, punched. Kicked. Again and again. Between slurs in Greek Kypriaka. Until gashes became bloody, until there was only blood.

'I've been here for practically all my life. My dad has Greek nationality, but he was born and raised in Lebanon. My mother is actually Lebanese through and through but both my parents have mixed origins. My dad is part Syrian, as well, and my mum is part Egyptian, both from the maternal side. My father's father lived in Constantinople and when the Istanbul progrom occurred in 1955 against the Greeks, he fled through Turkey down to the Levant region (I don't know if it's appropriate to call it that anymore). Anyways, he met my Grandmother on that journey. And they fell in love. My mother's parents, they are both Lebanese, but my grandmother was born in Egypt. She grew up there in an aristocratic family and then as we know all the Europeans and foreigners got thrown out of the country and their family, like all the others, pretty much lost all their wealth with that. Grandfather and Grandmother met when she was visiting Lebanon. She met my Grandfather, they fell in love. The rest of the story is in Lebanon until my parents came into it. Or I guess out of it. My parents were forced to decamp at the break of the war.

My parents hold a very strong pride regarding Lebanon. They also hold a very strong sense of pride of the colonial idea of Lebanon. Before the war, the country was known as "Little Paris" or "Little Switzerland of the Middle East". It was a very rich, very powerful financial sector. The New York Markets would only open after the Beirut markets would. It led the markets of the States. When we were growing up they didn't want us to associate with the Eastern World or at least the Gulf World, they wanted us to associate with the Western World and, therefore, they only taught French at home.

A lot of Lebanese Christians do not identify themselves as Arab. Having that need to say, "Oh, I'm not Arab. I'm Lebanese." It's very nationalistic. They will tie this back to their roots and say, "We're Venetians. We're not of Arab origin." This, for them, inherently holds a Muslim tie. They hold that difference because it means something to them having survived a war, civil war and mostly with people of Muslim origin. They grew up in a community where everyone was OK with each other. Then one day to the next everyone you knew to be your friend, family friend or everyone who had a different religion was your enemy. You couldn't trust anyone anymore. People had to stick to their religious community.

My parents are not going to act out what they think with people, of course. They treat everyone with the respect that they expect people to treat them with but open the conversation about people in the family my dad's first words are usually, "They're all Muslims. They're all shit. All of them, there is no difference between them." Despite knowing that the Muslim religion has its own denominations and separations. All of them are very different like Christians. You have so many different Christians. They will still lump them and say, "We know them to be like this and this is how they all are and so you can't trust them. You can never trust them." And they won't. They might like them a lot, the individual, the way they are, think that they are a very nice person but they will never consider them close or trust them enough to share something.

For us, as Lebanese Christians, we hold grudges toward the Palestine communities and the Syrians. Because when the Palestinians had their fights with the Israelis, we accepted them into the country. We welcomed them but instead of being grateful they brought us trouble. They started fighting us along with other Lebanese Muslims. That's when the civil war broke out. Then the Syrians came in to "calm everything down". We hold a huge grudge against the Palestinians and the Syrians and a lot of hatred towards them for this. Lately it has changed. From my generation onwards they've changed a lot. Mostly because of the awareness of racial discrimination. But still. It is ingrained.

My parents suffered a lot. It is understandable they hold that perception because they suffered so much. You're talking about friends and family dying. All of my uncles fought in the war and all almost died. One of them has a crater in his neck from a bomb because a piece of shrapnel hit him and went through the other side and he survived that. So, you can understand why they're so harsh with nationalities that were involved in the conflict. But on the other hand, they hold a colonising perspective of the world, which is why they pushed us, my siblings and I, towards that view rather than pushing us more into the roots of the nation itself. It makes my parents sound really bad but they are not bad people. That was one of my growing up factors of dealing with my nationality between Lebanon and Cyprus.

Funny fact is that the Cypriot people are not just tolerant, they are very tolerant and accepting of Lebanese people, especially Lebanese Christians. When Lebanese were leaving their country during the war, they were coming with very very large suitcases with gold and money, which they invested here. What a lot of people don't know was soon after when the invasion happened here in Cyprus, a lot of the Greek Cypriot communities started attacking a lot of the Lebanese Christians living here and taking their money because there was a shortage of food, of money, of everything. These things don't get talked about. And yet, there is this loyalty from the Lebanese community towards the Greek Cypriots .

Another essence of loyalty is sympathizing in their sentiments about the war, and part of it is feeling the conflict is part of me as well. This is why it is so hard for me to cross the border (with North Cyprus) and I have only done it once, last year. I was forced into it. It is so hard to explain why the border was and is such a big deal for me. It was kind of like crossing a boundary, breaking a limit. Something that I wouldn't normally do but I did. I got out of my comfort zone for it. I feel like it was a huge step for me. Coming from an area that has huge conflict, you're bound to grow up with some hatred for someone because that's how the world is in this area today. It gave me a chance to step out of my own skin and start thinking about other things I've been biased about and rework that in my own mind. I felt alienated purely because I feel like it's this idea that's set in your head. Because you have this zone of emptiness where there is, like gates in-between. You don't have a hard time crossing physically but it gives you a feeling of crossing a border. We are conditioned to, I don't mean just Cypriots I mean anyone, everyone really, it's a pattern in our life. When you're crossing a border there are gates, there are things at an airport or whatever. You know you're going somewhere else. That kind of shifts your perception a little bit.

The moment I stepped over there I felt very alienated. The fact that I didn't understand or recognise the language made it even worse for me. So, when I came back my reaction was, "Ouff, I'm home". Which kind of sucks because technically that's home as well. It extends that way but people can't and don't see it that way. My experience was walking around the old town a little. Sitting at a café and refusing to buy anything and just making my way back here. The reason why I don't spend anything and won't spend anything there for now is because to me it's inappropriate. I don't do it out of disrespect of the people over there. On the contrary, if there was some kind of, I don't know, federation or if they did have their own independent government that did not rely on Turkish help and providence, then I'd be happy spending over there. But as long as there are foreign soldiers and they are under Turkish jurisdiction…I don't want to get into the politics of it, basically. Knowing my own family's history, I am a little biased. Not a little, I'm very biased. I still hold a lot of reserves. I haven't been back since.

Growing up, I was always a little more isolated. My friends were all foreigners who were migrants here like me. I never learnt Greek till I was half-way through high school and that was part of the reason for struggling to befriend Cypriots. They would laugh at me, saying, "You are Greek but you don't know how to speak Greek." And I would get into fights a lot with the local children about my foreigness, about my speaking English but also about stupid things they would do. They had this attitude that they were better, and I guess it didn't help that I had my own sense of right and wrong, justice. Of knowing who I am. I grew up in a very religious environment. My family is of the Maronite Church. It is part of my identity but so is conflict, so is being part of a family that does not go to a family's village on national holidays or on Sundays, but instead does its own thing. But we, as a family, all feel ourselves here, here is where we have found comfort. And here is where we have found a home. I have done my best to integrate by learning the language in the last few years and maybe, maybe that is why I have been able to find so many native Cypriot friends now. I am showing I want to be part of their island. But I am not giving up who I am. Or saving myself from telling others what is right, what is wrong, even saving myself from them. I tell them who I am.

Whoever I am.'

It would have continued for the 'xeno' if not for a woman's voice, calling, maybe for dinner, maybe for an appointment, or maybe she had finally realised her eleven year old boy had been out of her sight for far too long and he was obviously up to no good. The group of boys left their neighbour on the tarmac, still breathing, barely, eyes fixed away from those leaving him behind. No, Julien's eyes were fixed on that body still hanging from its chain. Its fur matted and wet. Its eyes large. Fixed upon the moon. *Full moon tonight.* Even after the boy rolled over to his side, and crawled to the small body, the eyes did not move. After all of that, there was no longer a thing to save. *So much for being a superhero.* The kitten was dead.

Fear

I am RASHAD

'I am not scared. Why should I be?
Why should I be scared of scared?'

"'Frightened ?" repeated the boy.
"What does it feel like to be frightened?"'
'The Boy Who Found Fear At Last'
Turkish Fairytale

What is fear and how do we find it? Is it something we can dress or undress, address or redress? Something to wear or wear out, and then have to buy over and over again, spending the resource of ourselves to feed and maintain it? What should we fear, whom and why?

What if there was no fear?

WAR ZONE

Rashad was born, just as his parents had been in their time, in Iraq. He traces his ancestry to the sands of what was once Palestinian territory. In 2003, under the presidency of George Bush, a US coalition invaded Iraq. Rashad's family was forced to flee before their family was forced to enduredthe same fate as the hundreds of thousands of civilians that fell victim to ruthless bombing. The family settled in Syria, temporarily, before the state erupted with its own conflict in 2011 against the Assad government.

'In Syria when there was war, I was scared. I was only ten years old. It was normal that when I am sitting and I listen to

bomb or gun somewhere. Not normal but "alright, stupid guys". I was scared but it happen again and again and now it feels normal.'

Nothing. Feel nothing. Feel no fear.

'So now, here in Cyprus, if someone came now with a gun I would not be scared because what is he going to do, take the gun, put it to my face and say, "I want to kill you." I know how to touch the gun and move it. I found out how to do these things, dangerous yes, but I am not scared.'

THE BODY

The family later emigrated to Turkey. Though they were able to escape the war zones antagonising the Middle East, the struggles of the family were not over yet.

'My father was in politics. But he was sick after the war. We wanted to leave (Turkey earlier) but my father died and we had to wait.'

PASS THE TIME

'You know Google Translate? Before five years in Turkey, I don't know English and don't know Turkey. I had to talk to the kids, so I was writing "hello" there and it came "Merhaba". I was copying it and writing it on Facebook for some of the kids. Then I started to remember. I stopped copying them and I start writing them because I see them everywhere.

People use their phones just for fun. But there are other ways. Videos, nice programs. The media is important now. But the people my age they don't care. They look at me and say, "Oh my god look at this guy." But I look at them and think they are weird because next year you will see they did nothing. I will see myself, I did everything. It's like that.'

CYPRUS

'I had no idea about nothing. The people when they see us, all they see is people wearing hijabs and stuff. Not all the people but a lot. One time my family was walking home at night and these guys drive past. They were drinking beer and they throw at us bottles. At the Arabs and they shout at us how we Arabs. It was weird. First week that we were in Cyprus. It was like, oh my gosh Cyprus is like that.

The first time I went to school, I had no idea about nothing. People there from Greece, from Cyprus. I was the Arab there. I didn't know English, nothing. I was alone.'

PEER

'Some people with my friends was talking and they ask me, "Where are you from?" Like one girl she ask me, "Where are you from?" and I said, joking, "I am from Sweden." And you can see from her face she was like happy. And then after I said, "No, I'm joking I am from Palestine." And she changed her face, I don't know, she didn't like it. More people are like that. But from my character I do not talk to a lot of people. Just "Hi, how are you, I am fine."

I also played football. I went to some coach. It was my birthday, 25th of December. I was with my friend actually and my friend broke my leg. Playing football. He don't know he broke my leg, it become just hard. I can't feel it. The coach just said, "Oh just go home and put ice and it will be alright." I said my leg is broken. But he don't believe me. The people, the team, didn't care nothing. When I was playing there, they said, the people, it was all Cypriots and I was alone there. And everyone was talking about me, "Oh my god this Arab guy. He weak and crying about leg." The other people were not playing with me, I was playing alone. They ignore me and play together. I went alone home on my birthday. With a broken leg.'

THE NEIGHBORHOOD

'I was learning how to if someone has problems what to do (First Aid). And it happened. Four-three months ago, I was going to home and I saw one woman and two kids, she was alone. She was sick or something. I was like, I know what to do. I check the blood, the eyes. She had problems. Other people came and called police. It was hot, the sun, it was because of this and I tell people and her. She was OK, I was with her and she was OK. I help her and she say, "Thank you."'

RELIGION

'There are a lot of Muslim people in Cyprus. And the Cypriot character is not different from Muslim character. They and we can live together with Christians. Like next to my house has Orthodox Church. There is no problem. Not hating people like some people they go, "These people can't understand what it is like." No, it's not like that. Like about hijab. It's your life. I will tell you why I am thinking like that to wear or not wear. In the media they said that the Muslims hate the women or that they think the woman is nothing but no. Like my mum she born me. Of course, I respect her. Not wearing a hijab she will not be a bad person.

The Jews have their synagogue on one street. Every day I walk by it, I have my school there, so I see them. The Jewish guy, I will not hate him because he did not kill us. Maybe others in Palestine but I don't know where this guy is from, I am not allowed to hate him. Even the Palestinians they did bad things too to the Jews.

Christians sometimes said other people are going to hell. Some Christian people said the Muslim people are going to hell. But if

I know I am good, I will not go to hell. If I know myself, I will keep going.'

THOUGHT

'I wrote before. Every day. Maybe I will try to write again. It's nice you remember what you did today. Like sometimes I did nothing so I write nothing. "I did nothing today." And again, next day I write "nothing". Or in my program, even if I do nothing, I have to write even if it is "nothing".'

FEAR

'I am not scared. Why should I be? Why should I be scared of scared?'

Fear, where is it? Maybe Fear, or points of fearlessness, should be there by the fountain on Finnikoudes, the beginning of the Palm Promenade. Maybe that is where fear should be loitering, staring as you walk by. But instead, you walk on by, head turned, your gaze focused ahead. Because it has already happened, you have already seen Fear's eyes, and no more needs to be said. Do nothing. Fear, it's like that.

I am ALBAN

I've lost time and I'm losing hope.
This will be the end of me.

'I don't know how you are going to put this together.'

Those were my exact thoughts during our conversation. Sitting on a bunker in Alban's room, inside one of the steel containers at the Reception and Asylum Center of Kofinou, my eyes wandered from the hunched man sitting on the stool before me and the rest of the room. The mattresses propped up or still lying on the ground. The clothes piles in every corner. A bag of rice and turmeric. A plastic bottle of water. A bar of cheap soap, still dripping. One man lay on another bunker, staring at his phone as if reading but the screen was dark. There was nothing to see but his own outline. I turned back to Alban. He lit a cigarette, the second, and the smoke rose but had nowhere to go. The barred windows were shut and the door closed. The smoke rubbed against my eyes, my nose and my clenched jaw. I tried breathing through my mouth, imagining the gas particles entering, their bodies maimed with carcinogenic scars that touched the sides of my throat and grasped at the flesh, creating lumps, blockages. I tried not to look at the picture on the cigarette packet. Instead, I swallowed. It was the least I could do. The other man did not care; at one point he rummaged through his own pack of cigarettes but found it empty.

'Albania is my birthplace. As a child, I was very progressed in my thinking from everyone, even more than my teachers. This was because of my family. Even though we were very poor, if you

can imagine we didn't have anything to eat a lot of times, neither my father or my mother made enough money to feed the whole family, they would buy a magazine called Fatosi. They bought it from 1987 onwards. This was about everything the Communist regime did not want you to learn in school. I learnt everything from that magazine, even at such a young age.

You have to understand, I grew up in the communist regime of Albania. Whoever was against that regime or if someone demanded their human rights or who wanted to be like Europe, the regime slaughtered them, they hanged them all, they took them to prison. When I was fourteen years old, I got into trouble. I was trying to work a little to help my family. But I got into a fight with another guy at the site. I was defending myself but, unfortunately, that man died. I had to go to prison for three years even though I was just fourteen but the authorities had nowhere else to put me. So, I went to prison.'

There are at least another five men that sleep in this room. It's a tiny space. When night comes, each lies frozen still. One movement and they will hit their neighbour. But who can talk of stillness and peace, when each man sees nightmares, reliving the horrors of their recent lives? Twisting and turning, soundless crying and heaving wails, sweats despite the full blast of the AC. That smell.

Five men sleep in that room, but all five do not sleep.

'The communist regime came to power under Enver Hoxha and he was the worst and biggest Dictator the people of Albania had ever seen. I don't think there has ever been a bigger dictator than Enver Hoxha.

I was freed from prison in 1989. I was taken to do difficult manual labour at seventeen years old and then I was recruited into the army. I didn't want to serve this regime but they forced me into service. I hated them all, all the officers who were all hypocrites. But then I met one of the officers who was different. I had a lot of respect for him even though he was a communist. He was the only one who was an actual communist unlike the fake Enver Hoxha. He praised me for believing in democracy, but he told me to keep it quiet and follow the Law. He said this because he didn't want anything to happen to me. The Hoxha regime would silence me permanently in the ways that Stalin did to his people or Hitler. So, I knew I had to flee Albania. There were two other soldiers who didn't want to serve under this regime. But they were afraid. I couldn't persuade them to escape with me until I started threatening them. I told them if they didn't come with me that they would be punished by association, that they were already under the "Bad Eye" and black list.

We found a way to flee to Greece in the beginning of 1990. When we were safe, I began attending one of the American colleges in Athens. Just before I was to graduate, the school was shut down in 1975 and, because of this, I wasn't able to get my diploma. Greece's economy at the time wasn't doing as well as the rest of the countries around it but when I left Albania, Greece was doing much better than my birthplace. But I always had the thought to return to my country when I was there. Something is always pulling me back to Albania.'

He stands up. Slowly, he walks to a makeshift closet at one end of the room. There are piles of things inside, boxes of personal hygiene, keepsakes and gloves, T-shirts with stains and jumpers that look fresh, folded up jeans and crumbled trousers, a smell of dried sweat and another, bitter. Alban takes out a suit draped over the sole hanger, and dusts it off. He then turns to show it to me, proud, pressing me to feel the sleeves, the pockets. It is not just the material he wants me to admire but also the tags, the brand names just barely visible after all these years. He stresses the brands, the retail price of the suit. He had bought it at its full price. This, he insists, marks him out from the rest of those in the room. From the camp, from everyone at the centre. This, he , makes him real, a person of quality. Feel it, he repeats, I am here, this is me. Genuine silk.

'I married. I will tell you the truth, I'm Catholic. When I returned to Albania after Greece, I saw her with her mother and fell in love with her at first sight. I have no words to say how much love I had for her. We had three kids, but I was always working abroad. I worked two shifts to support my wife, kids and myself. I could see that life under Communism was stressed, there was too much hunger. With the wage I earned I wasn't able to buy plain bread. I once again decided to leave Albania. At one point I made it to Switzerland and I asked for asylum because things were getting harder. Once my son was old enough, I thought to take my children to Switzerland where there was a better economic situation. I worked day and night. Finally, I was able to bring my family over. When I took them to Switzerland, something went wrong with my wife. She went mad. At that point, someone was after my life, I know they were, and my wife didn't believe me, the police didn't believe me, no one believed me. So, I had to run away in secret, leave my family alone in Switzerland. There was no other way.

I went to Belgium to save my life. In June 2013, I asked for protection there. Whilst I was there, they came for me. They, those who wanted my life, I cannot say why or who they were. Just they. They found me easily, following me from Switzerland because I brought a phone from Switzerland and they found me from the location on my phone. I was at a bar with a group of men, we were sitting outside talking about the politics of Albania. Countrymen of mine. Then we saw the car coming towards us and it changed its lane to the wrong lane. I said to my neighbour that the driver must be drunk. Another said that it must be a robbery because he could see guns. The people in the car aimed their guns and the aim was towards me. They did not have masks. I saw their eyes, their faces. They looked up and saw the cameras on the street and I think that is what stopped them. The cameras saved my life. As soon as they drove past, we called the police and told them that someone tried to kill me. The police at first didn't believe me. Finally, they believed me and said that I needed to be brought in for protection. They took me to the police station.

"We need to keep you here until 7am. We need to find you a house and change your name."

I was suspicious and so afraid that I decided to leave Belgium with a Macedonian friend and head to Helsinki, Finland. I applied for asylum there. Three months later I was contacted by Switzerland to return to their territory. I said, "How can I go back? I'm trying very hard to free myself of those people who want my life and you're taking me to death?"

"Sir, this is the law of the European Union. You must return to the country you first asked asylum from."

I was taken with an armed escort from the Finnish police to Switzerland. When I arrived in Switzerland the authorities just left me. Unprotected, vulnerable. Usually they would take us to prison. But like this, leaving me, I had no protection at all. This is what they had planned. Like a fish on a hook.

My wife, she had the devil inside of her then. At first, she wouldn't let me into our home there in Switzerland. Then she demanded I take her to Albania to see her sick father. Even though it was dangerous for me and I was legally not allowed to leave Switzerland, I accompanied her in 2012. But what she did there…she was so harsh. The woman whom I had loved so much. I had a sum of money that I had saved up in case she or the children ever got into trouble and I was not there for them. She never told me that she wanted to return to Albania to steal the money then hide from me. I had worked for twenty-three years nonstop for this to give to my family so they wouldn't have to suffer like I did under the communist regime. She stole from me. I followed her back to Switzerland, trying to find answers.

One morning, it was Monday at 8 o'clock, I had recently arrived. I was called into the Swiss police station and was arrested. "You're arrested!"

"For what reason?"

"We'll tell you."

I was arrested under the allegations of mistreating my wife and children. I'm in an area of Switzerland where everyone knows everything about everyone. I was imprisoned for 28 months even though I was innocent. They said, "We know you. We know you're innocent but…"

"How can you let a person be imprisoned for 28 months if they are innocent?"

At this time they were listening to my ex-wife. It was just a trick to put me into prison, to delete me as a person, a punishment from my wife for my not earning enough. And the Swiss police fell for her lies. Every country told me in their own way, that they wanted to help me but it wasn't in their best interests unless I sold some valuable "favours". I was, am, will be punished for my silence.'

He shows me his scars from where bullets had passed, the leg that still causes him intense pain. He has no photos beside his mattress but his own body, a memory enough. Caught within it like in the room, not able to squeeze out of its walls, holding onto a belief of a future, that seems incongruous against the dampness and mould in the top corners of the room, the dissolution of privacy even as he tells his story. The words he uses have to step over the rest of the bodies lying around the room, hopelessly hopeful, scrolling through phones, staring at the possibility of Facebook and Instagram. In the faith of a world outside the gates of Kofinou. The fences of their own imagination.

'Let's go forward. When I was in Albania, 11 July 2016, I was banned from stepping into any European country. Every country I passed through they caught me on camera and they all said that they knew who I was.

"We should imprison you, but you need to go. Flee!"

Lots of times they let me leave. July 23, 2017, again I was shot in the leg. I believe it was because of my opposition to the Albanian President. They didn't cut my leg off but they replaced it with metal. I could just about walk with two sticks. I mortgaged what I had, for 2000 Euros, to escape to Cyprus to get my bearings. I paid for the ticket in Kosovo.

I arrived in North Nicosia and was in shock because I thought Lefkoşa was Greek, not Turkish. I arrived here and they asked me how long I was to stay? I asked if I could stay for as long as I wanted. They said no. So, I got a Taxi from the airport to the Green Line. I didn't want to stay in the Turkish part. The Turks have been the enemies of the Albanians for a very long time. I could never live there. They had us for six hundred years as slaves. What kind of face would I have to ask my enemies for help?

I thought and always said that Cyprus was our good neighbour. I believed they would help me with something. My taxi from the airport to the Green line cost me fifty Euros. I got to the checkpoint. I gave my passport and I thought they would not let me pass. I am not European, no visa for the South side. They checked my passport again and again. They said I was fine, that I could go. I said, "No, I want the ambassador. I want protection." They asked me if I wanted to stay anywhere.

"I don't care, only that I'm by myself for health reasons."

They said they will find me something. They brought me here to this. To this "camp".'

He is tired but leads me out of the room. As soon as we are out, the fresh air hits me hard. It is still raining or spitting as is common in Cyprus. But even the chill of droplets is a welcome after the little room. My own claustrophobia. The smoke. We walk towards the entrance/exit. He points out the bathrooms that do not work, the kitchen that is not safe, the sewerage overflowing. It is December and, whilst the outside world prepares for the New Year, there are is no festive spirit among the residents here. There are people everywhere, sitting, wandering around, just standing around but hardly anyone notices us. There is a daze, a frozen spell they all seem to be under. Caught under a bow, a frown that they cannot escape.

'I am sorry I am not very happy. I don't have the energy to tell someone, "Kali Xronia" or "Happy New Year". I can't say it. I should have a nice house. I am in a European country. How can you wish someone a "Happy New Year" if that person hasn't got bread to eat? From what soul, from what heart can you wish them a "Happy New Year"? I feel like whoever does so here is making fun of us. A wish is a sacred, holy thing. If you say it with only your mouth and not from the heart then… what heart can wish these things on people? It's like you're lying to yourself. It's that much. That's how I see it. I hope hope hope something will change. If it doesn't change it will get worse each day. I've lost time and I'm losing hope. This will be the end of me.'

I am AMELIE & I am LANI

The 'friendship chain'

Sunday. A coffee shop. There are two women before me. They found each other through a friend of a friend of a friend. They call it the 'friendship chain'. It's how they survive here, they tell me later. Without it, they would be all alone. But sometimes they don't mind.

AMELIE

'I'm from the Philippines. I stay here for four years. I find that it is not quite nice but this is our life. We have to earn money so. In the Philippines, even if you earn this money, tax take away and you have little money. But my life in the Philippines when I small it's actually very happy. There in the Philippines is not the same as here in Cyprus. Because here in Cyprus people are selfish. In the Philippines they help each other. They can see... it's like if the rain is coming, they gonna help you. Each one is gonna help you, so that it's the work will be finished. When I was young, I went to school then when I was in a college I stopped studying because there wasn't a lot of money. My parents they work as a farmer. That was not enough so I have to go to abroad to go to help them. When I study, I study first year of college. I got teacher course, but in the end I give up to support my parents. Actually all my siblings they finished their study except me. I helped pay so they finish.

I go to Cyprus when I was nineteen. My parents take good care of me and gave me money but now I'm the one who give them money. I apply to an agent to come here to Cyprus. It is very expensive. I think here in Cyprus the money is nothing but for us it's 20,000 or more, some they pay 150,000 pesos (7000 Euros) just to come here in Cyprus.

I come to be domestic helper in house. For the first weeks it is difficult. I have to find out what they want. I have to find out what they do and what they don't. So first time it's really difficult because actually in our contract our work is 7 hours and we have rest also. But I work all day. All morning 6.30am to the evening at 5pm only my rest is to eat lunch, then continue working. That's the life of being a domestic helper here. It is very difficult. You have no choice, just to earn money.

We have curfew. We call it curfew. When you say you'll be back at this time, you have to. You have no choice. You want to stay with your friend, hang out with your friend. There is no choice. Because our employer tell us, "We need you, you have to come back at 5 o'clock." You have to. It's like when you're off on a Sunday and on your off day employer say, "We need your help." We have no choice.

You are alone here. The agent no care, get money then don't help you anymore. They just take the money the employer pay them and they don't care. They never ask, "How your work? How's everything? Is it ok? Do they let you rest?"

When I first saw my employer it was only an old man and a woman. So, I told them I keep on fighting my rights that they signed the contract and I should only work 7 hours. My old woman is very terrible. The old man is good. He is very good. Have kind heart. But she don't let you go on your off day for a whole day I have to get up at 6.30 and have to prepare breakfast and lunch before I go and I have to come back early. So, when he died I told my agent that I don't want to work with them. I have to find another employer and I have to take all the money that I had. Those holiday that they not pay me and I was working.

So, this the second employer that I have is quite nice now. I find another employer quickly. My first interview actually, I tell to myself to get out of that house. How I wish I have better life, good employer, not the same. The prayer was granted and now for one year that I stay to my new employer it is nice. It's a family and all these holidays I have. They give and I have actually 10 euro every Sunday. I have allowance. Extra. Sometimes they see I'm hard working they give me more allowance. 15 -20 euro for allowance on Sunday. My previous employer they are like, "What are you doing? Telephone, you cannot." My previous employer I could not hold my mobile till I finished my work. Here they hear my mobile is ringing and they say, "Your mobile is ringing. Stop that and go answer." It's more free. I have two hours, three hours, fours hours like that, it depends, if I iron clothes. I have more rest in the afternoon until we have dinner and that is all.

Yes, but it's OK because I only help them to prepare breakfast before they go to office. When they go, all the time, all the time is for me. It depends if I can work quickly I can finish my work early so I can rest. I eat with them even. It is like there is a reason for me to do something, they will let me stop that and told me to eat lunch, dinner. They want me to eat with them together. I feel like part of a family and we can joke with each other. If we are in the kitchen, we talk like a friend, like a family. Because my employer said that, the thing with us we know you work with us but we treat you as a family, as a friend. You're not just here to working, working. No. You are here for our family. So, I feel blessed.

Now I no talk to Cypriot outside house. Because I found out if Cypriot think that we are "Philipina" if you talk to the Cypriot they treat us like prostitute. That's what other Cypriots think. I would rather not. There is good Cypriot also but no. They think that we prostitute and buy us for little money. Yes, I don't deny it, some they do but some they not. So not all, they generalize all the Philippina here. In 100 person here, there like maybe 50 don't. I don't.

When I was new here, I have to make new friend, to teach me ways where I go. How to send money to the Philippines? I have to learn. But I tell you truth, I rather just stay alone because there's no true friend. Actually, the true friend is yourself. Because you know they do bad things actually. They talk about you. They make problem. They talk behind your back so it's nothing. Some Philippina, if they cannot get anything from you, you are like shit to them.

You can find out maybe one only, one or two friends. But you cannot find really true friend. The true friend is your family. So, don't trust. Now I don't trust anyone. Yeah, I can make girlfriend not that I give my totally trust. Like I don't give like last time because maybe they are good so I give 100% trust to them at the end. They don't take anything from me so, nothing. They just make a problem just behind my back so I don't need to make a lot of friends now. I can make a friend that I can make a friend hanging out like this but it's not that friend friend.'

LANI

'I'm from the Philippines. I am twenty-nine years old. I have two sons. Ten years old and four years old. I am married but we are no longer together. Going on three years. I am supporting my kids. They are staying with my mother. It is hard but I don't have choice to work in other countries for me to support them. Life must go on. The thing always positive in life because they are my inspiration so that's why I'm working hard for them. It's OK with me as a single mum as long as I know my kids are with my mother's care then I have nothing to worry about.

I think my mother loves them more rather than me. Before I work in Hong Kong but my kids before when I was in Hong Kong they're with their father. So, my mind before was not peaceful because I don't have communication with them. He cut communication with me and the kids. That is why when I come back from Hong Kong I get the opportunity to take them. The law in the Philippines is the mother has the right. Because my youngest is only four years old so automatically he is with me. My oldest son he choose me rather than his father.

Soon after I come back I need to go again to work for money. My kids understand. Maybe being a kid they want like, "OK, you go there when you go there and you have money you buy me like this, you buy me like that..." because children nowadays want more material things.

When I come here I try. I try my best but my first month I talk with the daughter of employer. The Yiayia, she no speak English, only Greek and I know no Greek. I said, "I cannot work long time because we're having problems. Your mother is always shouting at me when I don't understand her." Then her daughter tell me, "More patience. More patience." I do it but I'm not comfortable.

With Yiayia only problems. Even if I finished cleaning, if she didn't see me clean I need to do it again and watch me cleaning. It's like they don't trust us. They don't trust other people. They don't trust us. They just think that when they are gone, we play. We don't do anything. They don't trust me even little. When they need to go buy something from supermarket, I need to go also out the house, they will lock the house. I need to wait outside. Even 15 minutes, 20 minutes she will leave and I will go outside. It is hot outside. No shade. In summer it is very hot, and they go when very hot. I tell them I don't come here just to get your money or something in your house. I come here, I spend money to work. It is not comfortable they see me like stranger in their house.

When I'm cleaning her house, she will take her bag with her. Even when she is in the kitchen the bag is there. It's OK, take your bag. Your bag is safe. But me, I always said I will not get your things. That's how they see me.

They bring me back to the agency because think I steal. They told me to bring out all my stuff, my things, from luggage. I'm happy to, I bring it out and let them see one by one. Yes, I put one by one. The daughters looking at me and I said, "OK." I let her see my wallet, my bag, my phone, everything. When I tell them, "I want to leave, I want to leave, I want to go." They say, "You don't know what people we know in the Ministry. We will send you back to the Philippines anytime."

I'm like, "Oh my God, why? What did I do?" then I start crying because I'm scared. I'm only a helper, so they tell me like this for me to be scared. But this is our life.

I can't leave. If I have to go to another country, I have to find out what is their attitude. For now, I rather stay here to not make everything all new again. And what if worse? And with what money I go? I have no plan. I only work. My plan is for tomorrow to get up at 6am. Finished.'

As the afternoon comes to a close, the women stand up to leave. One is in a rush to return back to the house. Her curfew time is near and she still needs to catch the bus, which will hopefully not be late. The other has no extra money so she will walk. She will not accept lifts. For the whole 7km hike back to the house. Her only worry now is to be back in time before the door is locked and she will be forced to spend the night outside in the garden. They both walk out as the sun starts to set, lonely I think. Lonelier still when neither looks back to say goodbye, for goodbyes always mean the start to a new week. What good are they when they hurt.

Education

The ROMANOVICHES

If your outlook is positive towards a country, she will answer in the same way.

Mrs: *We lived four and a half years in Israel. My husband is Jewish, so that is why we moved there from Russia. Israel had its many perks. Israel is a rosarium for children. The nation loves children. However strange this may sound, it is very safe there. This is because safety is their priority. Wherever you are, you are surrounded by police officers, you just don't know that. In this way, you are not afraid to let your kids go out by themselves.*

Mr: *Also, the transport system. Yes, the transport is well developed. You just have to press a button and you can find your nearest bus stop, where you will need to change, how long this will take, when the next bus will come. So, from point A to point B it will take you 29 minutes 40 seconds, and this is how it will be exactly, not a second more or less. Everything is made for your comfort. Kids are able to move around freely, from one city to the next. The cities are very much like the cities here, like regions in Moscow. Or even smaller. It's a lot easier to move around. Not like Cyprus where even the taxis are a hassle to find, if you ever do.*

Mrs: *People are Eastern there, they are very kind. They wouldn't leave a person stranded outside. You can knock on any door and ask for a glass of water, they would open the door for you and pour the glass. This is something they have not yet lost. But they are very loud and, unfortunately, are not cultured or mannered.*

Mr: *But the cleanliness, it is much cleaner in Cyprus than there. When I first came to Israel, and I walked out onto the beach,* *there was a clear division between one part of the beach and the other. The one had Israelis and what seemed to be ex-Soviets who had been living in Israel for a long time and the other half also had our ex-Soviets, maybe tourists, maybe not, but who hadn't lived in Israel long, and other Israelis who had just arrived. The first group were eating roasted sunflower seeds, and all the shells were falling from their mouth onto their front, their clothes and all over the sand. Used nappies lie under the sunbeds, the kids were making towers out of bin buckets, because the bins were of no use to the parents. The other half of the beach, seemingly the same ethnicity of people, but they acted differently. The kids when called came to sit down to eat, then after eating, everything was packed neatly into bags and placed into the bin. All the ash from the trays thrown in on top, everything neat and clean. Why was that first group of Israelis like that and those others like this? They are setting models for their kids, which is scary, because the kids will mimic their mothers, their parents, how they eat, how they act. What are they going to grow into?*

Mrs: *I think this behaviour of the Israelis is known throughout the whole world. There are hotels who refuse to let out rooms to them. I am ashamed for them in these cases because they have become family to me. Israel is our second nation, now Cyprus is our third. But I don't want my kids to see that kind of behaviour growing up. Our eldest is already an independent character but the youngest, since going to school from six years old, so for two years, has now started behaving like a monkey. Children behave in ways that are most comfortable for them, so if they make something a habit, they will stop thinking about it and just act that way. What they see, they do. For example, where the bin is, if it is far, they will choose to throw their rubbish wherever. This is also one of those moments because it is so hard to fight this. Even some of our friends back from Israel, people who are educated, even* *they after smoking, they just throw their butts on the floor, and I ask them, "What are you doing?"*

Mr: *They say, "Damn it, I've been Israelised."*

Mrs: *There is already this kind of phrase. I don't want my kids to grow up thinking this behaviour is something normal. Shouting because everyone there talks in heightened tones although I wouldn't call Cypriots quiet. Israel also have a very alternative schooling system there.*

Mr: *The Israeli higher education is very strong but their primary and secondary schools are very weak.*

Mrs: *The system is they read to you, if you want to learn, you learn, if you don't, you don't. They won't ask you what you have learnt. That is the system there. When a child is school age, he can't organise himself. That is the system during university when lectures are delivered and even there, students struggle to organise themselves. That is the system and you don't have a choice. There are private schools but they aren't very different from the public.*

Mr: *It goes something like this. There is a class and the teacher calls a student to the board. The kid says, "I don't want to go up."*

"Why?"

"My head hurts." Or maybe "I'm not bothered."

And the teacher can't do anything, they can't force you to come up.

Mrs: *The teacher doesn't have any authority there. Unfortunately.*

Mr: *Because an angry mum will turn around and say, "Did you touch my child?"*

Mrs: *They pamper the children there. The biggest accomplishments in sports come from the ex-Soviets. Because those parents keep their children under control and push them.*

Mr: *And they occupy them with extracurricular activities.*

But the Israelis, "He is tired" or "Poor this, and poor that." They spoil the children and those children are allowed everything. Because, after finishing school, those children have to serve in the army. The boys for two years and eight months, the girls two years and four months. And the parents believe that in that way they give their children a real childhood and then the army will do all the breaking, disciplining. They don't bother doing it themselves for the eighteen years of their child's life.

Mrs: *This is the stereotype in their head. That the child will come out a different person after. The kids don't want to study after they have come out because you come out as a twenty-one year old, and very few go onto university. Over there it is quite normal for you to only start university at thirty and finally wake-up. After finishing the army, they almost definitely opt to go for a year to Thailand. They get a sum of money for their time and go crazy. "I am tired." Pshhhhhh.*

The reasons we left are quite a few. I am against war and against serving in the army. My eldest son was nearing the age of being called to army service and I didn't want him to serve there. Well, I don't want him to be forced to serve anywhere. I would rather he spend more time studying. Not in Russia, maybe Cyprus. Unless he chooses to do so, of course. Next, we were completely unimpressed with the education provided in Israel. And, so, we began to think about our eldest son who at that moment was fifteen and was about to turn sixteen. At this time, I suddenly had the desire to go on vacation to Cyprus. With my husband only. My husband supported the idea and whilst we were preparing, we also got the idea to find out about the situation of English schools and Holiday Language Camps in Cyprus since my eldest is always travelling to a summer camp to improve his English. He had been to a camp in the outskirts of Moscow, but it was not right. I also thought that from Israel the flight to Cyprus would be nothing, and we decided to do some research whilst we were there. Maybe even a boarding school.

So, we booked a hotel room and decided to combine our vacation with research. We googled private guides in Cyprus. We contacted one who was out of the country and recommended his colleague. The most important moment came, which was the meeting of the first person to introduce you to the country. That first acquaintance is very important, especially in how they will present this country to you. Under what sauce. And the guide did it beautifully. By the time we returned to Israel, we knew all the terms and conditions of relocating to Cyprus. We told our eldest and he, like any teenager, said of course I want to leave you and live there. Everything was perfect for him. Independent life from his parents? Yes, please.

Mr: *By then an idea was ripe in our heads. After making the necessary calculations that with sending a child over we are spending a specific sum, we will be travelling, he will be travelling back for the holidays, all these expenses, and with so many schools to choose from over there in Cyprus, our conclusions were that with that money we were going to set aside for our eldest's boarding school education, it would be enough to live on for the whole family. So that our youngest son could be educated there too. We didn't want to separate them and it all came into place.*

Mrs: *So, the decision was made quite quickly that we were all moving here. There was nothing holding us in Israel.*

Mr: *I had sold the business, so we were pretty much living there like tourists on holiday. I had opened a restaurant on the beachfront in 2014. There were a lot of tourists at that time. My restaurant was totally dependent on the tourist season. I opened my restaurant and in a month the war started. And so, of course, there were no more tourists.*

Wife: *At first, we were being bombed for fifty-one days. I took the kids and went to Russia whilst my husband stayed to protect* *the business. The conflict was called "Operation Strong Cliff". The first rocket came past on the 7th of July. It was the peak of the tourist season, the kids had only started their school holidays. They finished school on the 30th of June. All the tourists left. The restaurant had to close. Even for the locals, the grandmas who usually came out with their grandchildren would not leave their homes, everyone was sitting in their shelters. Israel has a great Iron Dome. It fires missiles to blow these rockets away, so they don't fall on our heads. We may only get the splinters. People experience this constantly when they live in Israel. The children are taught what they need to do in case of an emergency, what to do if they find themselves outside. To be honest, and as strange as it may sound, it may be unpleasant but it wasn't the first reason for our leaving the country. People tell us they wouldn't dare visit us, it's too scary for them but for us it became part of our life. Normal almost.*

Mr: *And you can understand them. You work the whole year, save your extra money and you get two weeks off from work so you can have a rest. You wouldn't choose a nation where 1) it is very expensive and 2) you don't know if there will be a war at any moment. And 3) you have crazy Arabs who are running around Jerusalem chased by the police, running around with knives. It is enough to come once to see Jerusalem, Tel Aviv, to all the sights, the Dead Sea. This is how I would do it, spend a day in Jerusalem, the Wailing Wall, walk by the Dead Sea and after that just put a tally over the nation. I've been there. Full Stop. Because it is very expensive. To travel there once is the same as going twice to Europe.*

Mrs: *Very true. And the high prices are not justified. The service is once again Eastern and pretty much not there. Why is there no service? Because the Israelis couldn't care less. They are satisfied with what they get. The expensive food at the restaurant is fine for them, the service that they get is something they don't* *notice. We, the Russians, are the ones who demand it because we come from a different mentality and culture. The tourists who come there just don't understand where all their money is going. But people live there, and they are very patriotic about their life.*

Mr: *Remember? A bottle of whiskey at a club cost us 300 dollars once. 300 dollars! We paid it but we expected some kind of show, some kind of service to be provided. We were contributing that much money into someone's business. A smile at least, you know. We were there to have a good time so give us a good time. But no, instead, the waitress couldn't even be bothered to come around to the VIP lounge. Where we were sitting, the section was raised above the rest of the room. She just threw the bottle over the barriers, and said, "Get it!" Not to come, pour it and take care of you a bit. No service. And yet she still expected tips for this. What tips? I am the one who had to pour it. Tips for what? Not even a smile.*

Mrs: *So, we made the decision to move. We arrived and everything started falling into place. The school, we chose the Russian school in Limassol in the end. And then it came to finding a place to live. My husband wanted a house with space and you could hardly find any in the centre of Limassol. I needed to be in the centre of town because I need life, civilisation, movement. I was set on a flat right by the beach. We were arguing over and over. Our guide made a call to an agent here in Limassol and within the time it took her to take us from Larnaca where the airport is and Limassol, this agent had found our perfect house. It was right in the center, two minutes walk to the port and beach and around the corner from the children's school. It was like it was meant to be. We had our minds set and in the right place and everything turned out smoothly, even better than imagined.*

When we began living here, we found there are a lot of similarities between Israel and Cyprus, in regards to their relations to Russians. How they react to us. They treat us as if we still walk in slippers and bear skins. I laugh at this. To think of Moscow and how advanced it is and everyone in their slippers and bears.

Mrs: *But some things are so different. The driving ...After 10 years of driving, I was scared to sit in the driver's seat for three months when we first arrived. You just can't understand what these Cypriot people are thinking whilst driving, I know the driving in Moscow, on the roundabouts, on the highway, wherever. I know the driving in Tel Aviv, I am not scared of anything. But here on these narrow roads and with the people behind and in front of you, I just don't understand what they want sometimes. But these are minor things. We have met so many good people that it feels like we have lived here forever. And under the sun, our children thank us that we can wake up every day, with joy for a new day. We can build a future for our children that we can be proud of. Beauty comes to the eyes of the beholder and in the same way, I believe, if your outlook is positive towards a country, she will answer in the same way. But if you are constantly unsatisfied with something, then of course you will have huge hurdles in your way. We didn't have any hurdles.*

I am OBI

Having a home country has no meaning to me anymore.

'My relationship to Iran was and still is a love-hate relationship. Actually, my relationship to Cyprus is a similar love-hate relationship as with Iran.'

Iran boasts of a long history of political oppression, most notably from the 20th century onwards. Between 1925 and 1979, during the reigns of the two monarchs, Reza Sham Pahvlavi and his son Mohammed Reza Shah Pahlavi, traitors to the regime were subjected to intense torture and executions. Even after the Iranian Revolution of 1979 and the Pahvlavi dynasty was overthrown, the climate for civilians did not improve. Indeed, the efforts of the later dictatorships merely heightened the terror within the state through the expansion of torture methods against prisoners. One of the most 'effective' torture techniques used to extract information from victims was with a contraption called a 'bastinado'. The 'bastinado', equipped with electrical cables, was strapped to the victim in order to shoot electrical waves across the individual's nervous system, an intensely painful procedure. An extremely painful procedure. Or, for a little variety, there was always the option of the 'Apollo', a helmet that was firmly placed on the head of the victim and would not only trap their cries of pain but reverberate them louder inside the brain, creating a seeming echo room filled with cries of agony, pleas for mercy. Many prisoners were shot dead in acts of vengeance by individuals within the armed forces, with no repercussions against the perpetrators. Throughout the 21st century, the state has been highly criticised over its violations against the human rights of its citizens both by national and international activists. Yet the violence persists.

'I was born in Tehran and grew up in Karaj, in a city close to Tehran of approximately 1.6 million habitants, until the age of 13. I am coming from a family with a political background. Before the Islamic revolution, my grandfather was involved in political activities against the Shah and had, therefore, been imprisoned for more than three years. After the revolution, my father got arrested because he was politically active against the Islamic regime. Our life was affected by this. Once you are against the regime, you will always have problems. No matter if you stopped being politically active or not. My father and other family members couldn't use any public services (e.g. insurance). My family was constantly under threat. We received threatening phone calls from strangers, people from the regime were breaking the windows of our house and telling my parents that they would kidnap me and my brother. Once every while they were taking my father for questionings. My father was mostly hiding in different cities, so the family was mostly separated.

As a child I didn't understand the political situation that much but was always curious to know more about it. I was feeling that something was not right. At home I could feel and hear the difficulties and horrible incidents happening to us and people around us. I also knew that, outside of the home, I should pretend that everything is ok and fine. One of the moments that got me into trouble at the age of ten was at school. The first page of every book showed the picture of the supreme and revolution leader Khomeini (as they say "Ayatollah", meaning "a sign of God"). Because of the talks at home, I made changes to his photo in every book and made him look like a demon. My teacher and the director of the school saw this and put me and my family into big trouble. I almost got dismissed from school and that would have meant that I would have had trouble to finish any education.

As time went on, living in Iran was getting tougher and tougher for us. We could see and feel that there was no hope and future for us there. There have always been talks in the family about us leaving to somewhere else to start a new life. But these were just talks and we never really thought it would turn into reality. We could never imagine to leave our home, our city and the rest of the family – especially me.

One day my father came home saying he couldn't stand this situation anymore. He said that we have to leave, but we had no idea where to. As a holder of an Iranian passport and nationality you don't have that many choices without issued visa. We did some research through travel agencies and found out that Cyprus is one of the countries which we could travel to without any visa. That was in 2000, when (tourist) visas were issued directly at the airport. We also realised that a UNHCR office (UN Refugee Agency) existed in Cyprus. This would make it easier for us to apply for a refugee status.'

The common definition provided by the UNHCR and similar bodies for a refugee is an individual who finds himself outside of the country of their nationality, in most cases, for fear of their or their family's life, and is forced to seek protection in another country. Oppression against the individual is usually based on the latter's gender, race, ethnicity, religion, sexiality or affiliation with a specific social or political group.

The Refugee Law passed in 2000 and adopted by the Cypriot government in 2002 focused on the 'principle of non-refoulement'. Specifically, on disallowing the return of an individual back to a state where their human rights and/or life are under threat. This legislation applied to all persons seeking international protection, whether asylum-seekers, refugees and/or their beneficiaries.

'My father left first, and we stayed behind. He took a plane from Iran and went directly to Cyprus. In the airport, he luckily got a tourist visa for two weeks and managed to enter the country. He stayed in Larnaca for a couple of days in a hotel we'd previously booked from Iran. He stayed there until he found the office of the UNHCR in Nicosia. He then moved to a room in Nicosia and applied for refugee status. From the beginning, he informed the refugee agency that his family should join him. After less than a year, our papers were fixed and me, my mother and my 8-years old brother could leave Iran by plane. Comparing our journey to one of the refugees who have to pass borders by foot or boats, I think ours had been somehow luxurious. I remember exactly the day of leaving. It was a sad and at the same time happy moment. Sad because of leaving everything behind and happy because of the new beginning.

I was born on August 21st and that's exactly the day we arrived in Cyprus. It was a completely new beginning. I remember getting outside of the plane and being hit by the boiling Cypriot August heat. We were happy to see my father, who came to pick us up at the airport. We took a taxi and went to Nicosia. On the highway, every tree we passed looked like a friend or family member we had just left in Iran. It was the first time I had left my home country. Everything was different: the language, the constructions, the people…it was hard to connect to the situation. I felt like a complete stranger.

We arrived to the apartment my father was sharing with two other men. He had his own room where we could stay. The first night was one of my worst nights. I felt very homesick, troubled, lost. I had trouble breathing and suffered several nightmares.

The next day, we went to the UNHCR office and fixed our papers. We got a residence permit as refugees but not yet refugee status. After the UNHCR office, we went to the Immigration Office and registered our papers. There, unfortunately, I got very disappointed in how people were treating us. The employees were very unfriendly and were mocking us. We stayed in my father's room for one week until we managed to rent an old house where we could move to. There, the locals and our neighbours were really friendly. Since the house was empty, they tried to help us and gave us some chairs, pillows and blankets so that we could have a place to sleep or sit. Thanks to the English lessons I had taken in Iran, I was able to communicate with them.

Back in time, there were no refugee camps, so we were lucky to live in our own apartment with a little bit of financial help from the UN. It was enough to survive. During this time, because of the Cypriot government policy we didn't have a work permit. I, of course, wanted to continue and finish my education. I had finished the eighth grade of school in Iran but wanted to do an A-level. Unfortunately, I didn't manage to get into the governmental schools because of my age and lack of Greek knowledge. For my brother it was easier. He had finished second grade in Iran and started going to a Greek-Cypriot school.

I went to the Ministry of Education in Cyprus and explained my situation but was told that to enter a governmental Greek class was impossible and that I had to enter private English schools. We, of course, didn't have the money to afford this. I felt helpless and I didn't see any chance for me to continue my education. I spent two years of my life sitting at home. There were not even any free Greek lessons to attend as they exist now. I believe that the Cypriot government didn't have any specific laws for the immigrants back then and that they didn't know how to handle our case. Back in that time, recognised refugees in Cyprus were usually transferred by the United Nations to other countries that were accepting refugees, e.g. Norway or Canada. Finally, after two years, I could join some free Greek classes and learnt some Greek, although it was still not enough to attend school.

I realised that I had to do something about my situation, since I had already lost three years. Then I heard from a family friend that there is a school in the Iranian Embassy offering classes until the A-level, mostly for the children of diplomats working there. I contacted the embassy and asked whether I could join these classes or not. I was told that the political situation of my father had nothing to do with me and that I could finish my education.

By learning the Greek language, communicating with the locals started being easier for me. Most of the locals were friendly and kind, but many times racism was pretty obvious. People were e.g. making fun of our nationality and our supposedly Islamic religion (although none of us are religious). Many times, they were asking hurtful questions e.g. if we had TV in Iran, if there were elevators and if I knew what an orange is.

Now, it is so hard to compare the two countries: Iran and Cyprus. It's like comparing two different worlds. When I left Iran as a teenager, I didn't care that much about the economic situation, but of course because of my father's situation, I knew that there was no freedom. When we moved to Cyprus, after some time, I could grasp the feeling of freedom and democracy. I started appreciating these things. But I haven't had an easy life in Cyprus. Having a home country has no meaning to me anymore. It's all about your comfort zone. Even after sixteen years, I never entered a comfort zone in Cyprus, because as a family we never got the option to settle down for good. Our residence permit got prolonged every three years, limited all the time, although we have been recognised refugees for the last fourteen years! Not to mention that we are also denied a Cypriot nationality!

So, do I think of Cyprus as my home?

No. No, I don't.'

I am THEA

It's not you! Don't take it personally.
*It's **them**.*

'I always wanted to be a social worker, a lawyer, or a nun.'

There is something about dreams that is consumed in want, wait and hope. We may sit in coffee shops and watch the world around us, the scuttle, the bustle or the emptiness of the streets, our hands engaged in the familiar: prayer, coffee or nervous table drumming. As we lean back into the chair's back, we may comfort ourselves in being at the edge of dreams, perching on the wall about to…jump or fall?

Thea sits beyond that dream. A woman of strong drive towards justice and a character that will not rest until every task in her diary is completed (to perfection). Even when sickness plagues her body, starves her hunger pangs and sleep habits, when the beating Mediterranean heat sends chills instead of heat jostling through her body, her tired eyes burn with an energy that is fueled only by modal verbs. 'I must', 'I will'. And she does.

'The Nun did not work out because I didn't think I could keep a vow of obedience. The social worker did not work out because I was afraid I would not be able to say "no" to people and put boundaries up. And the lawyer did not work out because I couldn't face defeat in court.'

Before moving to Cyprus, Thea had lived in some of the biggest metropolises in Europe. There, in the mass crowds, she could escape the *'small-town petty, gossipy, nepotism mentality'*. She had thrived in the webs of people going everywhere, nowhere. That is where she imagined her life to unfold.

Even after marrying a Cypriot partner, relocation was not in her or their plans. But as life happens, so does change and, in the face of family emergencies, developments are bound to ensue. The couple were forced to relocate to Cyprus. Thea's first introduction to the country was through the Immigration Services. *The Ping Pong Game.*

'Sending you back and forth, "Now bring another document", then "No, this is not the right one. I told you to bring something else." When I realised this is how you play the game, I asked the man for his name. I wrote on a piece of paper the requirements that he asked for me in order to apply for a Visa. So, when I came the third time and he said, "No, you don't bring the right documents", I showed him the piece of paper. "You told me this is what we needed and I got what you told me", and he said, "No, you didn't talk to me." I knew exactly I was speaking to the same person.'

Minutes accumulated into hours accumulated into whole mornings and afternoons in queues in the dim space of the Immigration building, waiting for an officer to see you. Under crumbling ceilings, beside peeling paint and across bleached floors, time moved and waited, and waited and move. There is only so much patience a person can practice when even the summer heat of the outside appears less oppressive than there, between the closed doors. Instead, there impatience, frustration and fury, voices raised, knuckles knocking against dented walls, a kick where many kicks had been. As the years passed, even Thea's patience wavered. She decided to apply for citizenship.

'I applied and two years later I was called to the office. That was two years then. Now it would be seven. Big room, 5 desks. A woman happened to be the one who took my case. She said to me, "Sorry, your request has been denied because your father-in-law is not Cypriot."

I said, "What do you mean my father-in-law is not Cypriot?"

"He doesn't have Cypriot ID."

"Yes, he does not have Cypriot ID because he has a British Passport, which he got when Cyprus was still a colony. But when you were taking my husband to the army, you said he was Cypriot because his father is Cypriot. Now I apply for a Cypriot nationality, you are telling me my father-in-law is not Cypriot? Anyway, what is the difference? I am not married to my father-in-law. I am married to my husband who has a Cypriot ID."

"Yes, but that is not good enough."

The other men who were sitting there were agitated by what they heard. So, that gave me the courage to stand up for myself. So, I asked to speak to the Superior. And the Superior came.

I said, "I don't understand what is going on here. This lady is saying no because of this and this."

He had a quick exchange in Greek with the lady from which I understood by the body language he was telling her, "Come on, don't make this difficult. It is a straightforward case."

She answered something in Greek. He looked at me, opened his arms and said, "Ehhh". This was another lesson in how Cypriot society works. It was obvious she had more power than him and the only reason why I have to guess is she was given the job by somebody higher up than the supervisor. That's how things work here. It is not what is right and what is wrong. It is who you know and what backing you have."

It was not only the smallness of the community, however, that began to choke Thea. The 'koumabaration' she could handle but the plague of the 'Mediterranean blood'. That was harder to close her eyes against.

'I remember walking home from church one Sunday evening and a car stopped and offered me a lift. I said, "No, I quite enjoy walking, thank you very much." He said, "No, no, no. You know what I mean by offering a lift." I was quite naïve, to be honest. I said, "I don't understand." He said, 'Oh come, you are young, I am young. We go together.' I said, "Sorry ,I'm married." And by that time I realise what's going on so I'm walking away. He said, "I'm

also married." The man gave me his business card with his name and telephone number. He said, "If you change your mind, call me."

Really, it was these times when I thought, "Is my skirt up?" and I thought, "No, I'm wearing trousers. Are they torn at the back and they are beeping because you know...?" I could not understand. I am talking about cars approaching from the back. I was not dressed provocatively, I was not wearing a mini-skirt. I was coming back from church, fully dressed. I thought, "Why, what is wrong with me?"'

Thea's first job was as a waitress at a nearby restaurant. Her experience there serving the male Cypriot customers, was an eye-opening lesson into the culture she would have to live within and without for the next twenty years.

'I saw the dynamic between men and women. It was really quite shocking, the sexual propositions of the men. The way they approached foreign women in terms of sex and expectations. Really, I felt like a piece of meat. I never ever experienced before anything like this. I was never talked to like this, in front of the wives as well. I was completely shocked how they treated their wives by flirting openly with me in front of them. How they were open with their proposals, it was really very sleazy and very unpleasant. But in my country if you have an extramarital affair, you would make it a secret. No one would know. Here, it's a reason to be proud of it. It's a reason to tell your friends. To be open about it. Flirt in-front of your wife? This was a very big shock for me.'

Years later, Thea would listen to stories that made her own experiences appear safe, child's play. Stories. Of simple people in complicated settings. Against simple laws that found themselves in complicated plots. Thea could not understand the connections between each feature within the narratives. How could a European country ignore or actively discriminate against individuals and/or groups of people within their neighborhoods.

'I thought no, there is something wrong with these people. Or they did something in the wrong way. They are not following the procedures. Because this is not possible. It's so illogical, it is so stupid, it's so obviously wrong. Out of compassion I would ask about a case and get very frustrated at the end because I could not believe that this was the situation. I blamed the actual people.'

How did it all begin? A friend of Thea's, who was working, asked her to step in as the contact person of seventeen women who had been the victims of trafficking. The friend needed to travel abroad urgently. It was supposed to be a 'just-in-case' position, if the women needed someone to talk to, not to feel alone in the world, in their suffering. Thea did not expect to receive any calls. But…

'She didn't make it out of Larnaca before the telephone started going off. Without knowing it, I was in it basically.'

Thea herself could relate to the women, on some level. Though these women faced and face situations of a more threatening and violent character, one that makes their stories chilling, Thea's own experiences provides women, especially migrants who have fallen victim to trafficking or abuse, with tools to become the active protagonists of their own narratives. Through her guidance and the support of Thea's tearm running their NGO, there are more stories starring heroines rather than a extended plot of victimhood.

'Now I'm meeting women who come crying saying, "What's wrong with me? Why are they doing this with me?" I tell them, "It's not you! Don't take it personally. It's not written on your forehead, it's not because of the way you walk or the way you dress. It's ***them****."'*

Team Spirit

I am NIGEL

That was the effect I had. I just walked onto the island and they noticed.'

'It's like a jungle, Cyprus in July, tree o'clock in the afternoon. I have just stepped off the airplane after a very early flight of four in the morning. It was raining in the UK when I left so I've got my trousers on, shirt. I turn up with my two suitcases and at the airport the guys picking me up have this big board with my name on it. I get into the car and it goes straight to Tekke.'

The area around the Hala Sultan Tekke was not the jungle that Nigel had first imagined. It was a desert with a small mosque. There was dust, sun-bleached rocks, two or three palm trees, discarded lizard tails, skulls of passed away animals, a cat, a rat, maybe a stray dog. There is also a trail that heads past the mosque and over a bank that is usually flooded in the winter and cracked in the summer. That pungent smell from the dried up Salt Lake, of something gone off mixed with something burning. There are sheep scattered across empty fields, munching on whatever is left over, maybe a few bent roots. Shepherds stare into the distance, red in their brazen faces, their eyes black holes as if they themselves have become the corners of the desert. There is no release from the elements, no shade from that sun. Only sweat. And it would only get hotter.

'The coach is there. The team is all there gathered, and they say, "Nigel, our team is here. Our manager is here. The committee is here. You say hello then you can go to your hotel and relax."

"Ah, wonderful."

But my coach then said, "You do training now, McNeil."

A run, 10 km, in this heat and I'm like, "Excuse me?"

There is a translator from English to Greek. I didn't know anything. I only knew swear words in Greek. The coach didn't have much English but they had a school teacher who was my translator. He says, "Nigel, we have your shorts. We know what size you are. Here are your training shoes. We start training in half an hour."

I'm like, "OK…" Didn't think we'd start running in the warm-up. 10 km. I think it took about an hour. I am at the back. I mean, I'm way at the back. It's me and the goalkeeper. And all I can hear is the coach shouting, "McNeil, run!"

I'm swearing in English. I'm calling him everything because I know he doesn't understand anything. I'm swearing in Greek and he's looking at me. I'm running. Each lap that I'm doing I'm shouting even more because I'm really really tired and I'm not prepared for this. I finished that day's training and I'm like dead. Totally couldn't move.

That first impression of Cyprus was really, really shit. All I could think was what the hell am I doing here? Am I so mad to be putting myself through all of this?

After, they dropped me off at the Golden Bay Hotel where I would spend two weeks. I had my meals and everything there although I'd just eat ice-cream because it was so hot. This stayed with me. The staff there used to go, "Double Ice Cream!" They used to shout it out to me. The people who used to work in the Golden Bay were Salamina supporters. It wasn't a little bit of ice cream but like wads of ice cream. Vanilla. I only like Vanilla. So, every time they brought me dinner there was always ice cream at the end. Then later they used to shout it out on the pitch and I used to know it was the guys from the Hotel. "Double ice cream! Double ice cream!" They never did learn my name, or they couldn't pronounce it.

Next came the trial. In the UK, when you have a trial for a team, it is a game trial. Not in Cyprus. Here it's a one-on-one trial, with a goalkeeper, with 400 – 500 people watching you. It's a training session, no pressure right? How all those fans knew I was there, I don't know. I just turned up, put my boots on. And I'm expecting to play a game.

"No, McNeil, you're gonna be with the Number One Cyprus player. He's the captain. He's gonna mark you. I'm going to pass you the ball. You're gonna take him on and shoot at our Number One goalkeeper." All this in Greek.

I'm like, "What? What do you want?" I didn't understand.

"You stand here. Other player there, goalkeeper here. I give you pass, you beat the player, then you score goal. Finish."

I'm like, "Oh, OK."

No problem, right?

So, I looked at the pitch. It was really bumpy. I could see everybody watching me and I had my Salamina stuff on. And I thought right, OK. I need to give myself space. I need to take the player all the way near enough to the box and then I will have all this space. When the ball will come to me the ball will be bouncing and I will not get good control. I don't want to look like an idiot. I don't want to look bad. I want myself to look good. So, I will give myself space. By the time he will pass the ball to me, I will be in a position for me to control it, turn and take the player on and score. That was my theory so I got the player behind me. I nudged him, actually I dug him, because when you hit someone, they go down. He was stunned a little so that gave me a couple of seconds to get off of him to take the ball. That was me playing football. I got the space I needed. I was in control, not him. The pitch was so bad, the ball was bouncing, bobbling. I went to take the ball around him, kicked it and it went straight through his legs. It was an accident. If I had planned that move, it would *never have worked. It looked like I meant it. He turned to me and went like, "You ****."*

Because, you know, you don't do that. It's disrespectful. It's like you're taking the mickey. That was the Number One player in Cyprus and I made him look like that in front of his fans. Like I was some big player. So, the ball went through his legs, I went around him and I kicked it into the top corner. I mean, it couldn't have worked any better for me. Everybody was going, "Woah! We've got a great player!", they're shouting out, "Panayia mou! Perrrrr! Mavro en kala!" The black guy is good!

Which was my moment.

I grew up in the UK. I was one of three black people out of 1100 kids in my school. So, you can imagine how popular I was. Which was a good thing for me because I played football so a lot of the players kinda knew me and had good relations with me. Before I was travelling from London to Harlow to play football. So, when my family decided to move up there I knew a lot of the kids from school. Growing up like a white guy and then every so often, "But you're black." But I live by this rule: if you have a problem with colour, get into sport because if you're good and you have white people next to you, they will support you. They will back you. They're gonna love you. I didn't face any racism. Didn't have it at all. I actually liked being a minority. I liked to walk in somewhere and people would take notice. Bring it on. I didn't mind.

My mum had been an athlete back in Trinidad and Tobago. She had been a sprinter. So, I think I got my passion for sport from her. My dad was a builder, an architect. In the late 50's, my mum and dad migrated to the UK… you know, they had ambitions. My dad worked in industry and construction, and my mum became a nurse. It was very difficult in the 50's and

60's for black people. The locals didn't understand and what you don't understand you are scared of, and when you're scared there are barriers. We had a big family. I started playing football at six and all the other children on my team were seven and nine years old. I became strong very quickly. When I was fifteen I got picked up by West Ham. I was there for five years, six seasons. Just off of getting a professional contract, my knee just went. I lost that contract. I carried on my studies until one day I got a phone call to come play in Cyprus. In '87, I moved to Cyprus.'

'I didn't speak any Greek and they spoke very little English so when I met the players of Salamina all I could hear was, "Da da da McNeil. Da da da McNeil…" I didn't know what they were saying. For the first five years I didn't understand anything. All I remember was my name there on the board during games and it was spelled McLee not McNeil. They couldn't even say my name properly. I even ended calling myself McLee because I heard it all the time. "McNeil or McLee, you go there there there and finish. Put goal." It was like that.

That first season I scored ten or eleven goals. Top scorer in the team and the most goals they've ever had in their league. It was at the time when Salamina started to get good. In the second year, I won the top scorer in the whole league. Top goal league scorer in the '89–'90 season. I was the first player for Salamina to do this. First black foreign player to do this for Salamina. I scored the 1000th goal in the whole of the Cyprus league. I broke so many records. That year I was the third most popular person. I was more popular than the president! It was a poll by a magazine. I still have it at home. Top of the poll was a singer, second was a model, and the third was me. The president was fourth or fifth so you can imagine how good my time at Salamina was.

When you play football in a village or town and this is very small playing in Larnaca, it is a completely different atmosphere from the pitches in the UK. It is very personal. Everywhere I went, someone supported my team or they knew me. I couldn't go anywhere, "Bloody hell Nigel, what you doing out?" It was very difficult. Didn't matter where I was, people would come up to me. I'd be sitting down, talking and they would come up to me saying, "Hey McNeil, what's going on here?"

"Hey man, I'm having a conversation here."

That's how they were. I think they loved me. I've got a friend of mine now–I'll never forget this–I've got pictures of him climbing the wire of the stadium to get in. I scored two goals against APOEL. The second goal he just went crazy. He's climbing the wire fence and it's about thirty feet up and he's at the top trying to get into the stadium to run onto the pitch. He's a fanatic Salamina supporter. He has his own business. The police surrounded him and he's still trying to climb in because in all those years the fans had never seen Salamina beat APOEL. And the way we beat APOEL. APOEL is like a big team. It was like Salamina against Arsenal or Liverpool. I came and within one season we're beating the big teams. It was like wow, we can really do this. I gave them this mentality. I hated losing. They were fighters, the team was, but they didn't know how to get it out of themselves. And because of me, I got it out of them. I got them to relax before the game. To visualise victory, to reach it. It was incredible.

Anyway, so I meet this same guy years later in these bizarre but common circumstances here in Larnaca. I walked into this Periptero (kiosk) and I instantly knew the owner is a Salamina fan. There were photos, the logo etc. The woman on the counter looks up and you should have seen her face. She was angry. I'd never seen her before but she knew me. She was like, "McNeil! I am fed up of your FUCKING name!"

I just walked into the shop to buy some juice. And I get this.

I said, "Excuse me. Why?"

"Every night, my bloody husband says, "Goodnight McNeil."

And I'm like, "What!?"

Turns out this was the guy who climbed that bloody fence. It was his shop and his wife. Then she said, "When you go into my bedroom, I have a picture of you."

I said, "What!?"

"My husband said, If you marry me you have to have this in the bedroom. This picture."

So, it turns out there's a picture of me next to the bed and every night, and I swear this is true, her husband would say, "Goodnight McNeil." And then the guy walked in five minutes later.

"Apanagia mou! Oh my God! McNeil!"

I had the juice in my hand, he was like, "You're not paying. You're not paying."

They still remember me and it's been over thirty years now. That was the effect I had. I just walked onto the island and they noticed.'

I am HAMEES

You just want to hear it and move on, hear it and move on.

It's hot. Even though the sun has long since tucked itself away for a well-earned slumber, the crowd is still sweating. There is vapor rising from their pores, through their T-shirts, into a cloud above their heads, between each other's bodies. The smell of salt, chlorinated skin, lavender-infused soap. Mint, and pineapple syrup, cheap wine. A lot of clinking glasses of ice, sipping out of plastic straws.

The older British couple drink their beer and whisky at one end of the bar. Their friends from Yorkshire, staying with them for the season, are tipsy enough to attempt karaoke, though how far they will go with Madonna's 'Like a Prayer' before they push each other off the stage will be something to look forward to. A group of Norwegian guys, tall and broad shouldered, are chatting up a group of German girls, practicing the little German they know. The numbers ('ein', 'zwei', 'drei'). The animals ('Schwein', 'Hunde'). The girls, mouths puckered, betray no return of affection. At the bar, one Hungarian is having better luck with two Russian ladies, though his pocket may not be saying the same after the third, fourth drink they order each. All of these moments may have happened that night, in the midst of the crowd swinging their hips, passing a joint now and then, Estonian, American, Kuwaiti, Ukrainian, Czech, Brazilian, panting, sweating, laughing, sweating, drinking in the sweat, dancing the night away, the good times that may be forgotten the next morning. Welcome to Napa, 1999.

At the front of the stage, Hamees gets a beat going, waves an arm at a buddy and nods his head as the tune leans in towards a more upbeat rhythm. His head is bobbing along with the crowd, and they follow along to his taps, breaking only to go buy another drink or cool off outside. Between one piece and the next, he takes a quick cursory glance across the room, breathing in the energy of the crowd, the inebriated good-spirits, and feels it seeping into his own. He lives for the summer, to feel life, of freeing yourself and making your time a good old joke, a laugh.

'Ayia Napa was fun because it was what I had seen on TV from places like Ibiza. I was like wow, I'm working in the center of tourism. The years I was up there were the best years that they ever had. People had money. People that came out there were nice. There wasn't a lot of trouble back then like there is nowadays. I always had this theory that why should I travel anywhere? Everybody comes here. So, what's the point of going on summer holidays somewhere?'

'My name is Hamees. People think it's Hamit. So, straight away they're like, "Where are you from?" and they always mistake me for being Turkish. My funny joke is when people tell me, where are you from?' I always go, I'm Lebanese Cypriot. And then they go, which part? and I go, sideways. And then they'll be like, huh?' I'll be like, yeah one leg and one arm. Half-half. But both my parents are Lebanese but I grew up here so I do consider myself as Cypriot.'

Hamees was born in Beirut, just before the breakout of war in Lebanon. With the ongoing conflict, and the tensions precipitating throughout the country, the family were forced to emigrate to Saudi Arabia where Hamees' father was working for a company. There they settled into a routine. The children started school, practiced Arabic and met their own hardships: bullying, belonging and brawls.

'I was in an all boy's school. 1200 kids. There was myself, a Chinese kid and an Indian kid who were the only three Christians and we were kinda treated badly because the others knew we were something called "Kafir" ,which was an "unbeliever". We were always picked on as kids, at a young age. I've got the scars to prove it.'

Every summer, the family would travel. One holiday getaway they enjoyed was on the nearby island, Cyprus.

'My dad loved Greek history and, while he was studying history in Lebanon, he made a lot of Cypriot friends. He was always throughout his life going back and forth to Cyprus until one of his friends told him, "Why don't you buy a house outside of Paphos?" Dad was in a new up-and-coming company at the time. The deposit for a new house in 1982 was 100 dollars. So, my dad was like, OK let's do that.'

In a series of unfortunate events, Hamees' father soon after became unemployed. The company he was employed at was liquidated. The father decided it was best to move the whole family to Paphos to the house he had purchased whilst he sought employment elsewhere. That is how Hamees' family ended up emigrating to Cyprus.

'Growing up in Cyprus was awesome, actually. We grew up in Paphos. Paphos was a touristic place so we had our own private pool. We could go down to the beach. It took us fifteen to twenty minutes to get to school. Because my dad was unemployed for a good four years, we did struggle a bit growing up but he did put us in an English school. He made sure that we were provided for.

I wasn't the brightest spark on the block. Anything that was scholastic, I tried to run away from but I adapted. I mean in the school, it's funny actually. You know the film Little House on the Prairie *where they all went to one classroom and the same grade was in the same classroom but you just moved up desks? Actually, the forth, fifth and sixth were in the same room. I remember it was two desks for the forth, two desks for the fifth and two rows of desks for the sixth grade. And it was the same teacher teaching us the whole thing. There were only like eighty kids in the whole school. From kindergarten to high school. I remember when I failed the fifth grade, all my friends moved up to the next two seats and I just stayed in the same spot. That's something my sister always made fun of me because she nearly went to the class. "What happens if I move to your school. Will I be in the same grade as you? You gonna fail again?" I was like, "Nah."*

Bullying? Well, it was the usual picking on. It wasn't so bad because everybody was a foreigner and that's what made it easy. Because there were South-African Cypriots, a lot of English-Cypriots. Different cultures. We had Germans, Irish. We had a mix. It was rare to have a full-on Cypriot kid attending the school and, if there was, then they were the minority. We were always kinda stuck together. You had your teasing, a little bit of bullying between friends. Funny enough, I didn't spend a lot of time growing up with Arabic people. It was always British Cypriot, like mixed races and cultures. It wasn't until the invasion of Kuwait, that massive one that happened, that we had a lot of Kuwaitis, and Jordanians, people that lived in Kuwait that would come and, like I said, we lived in an area which was touristic so they came for the summer but actually they ended up staying at school because of the war.

I was DJing from fourteen, fifteen. See, that's the thing. In Cyprus it's different when it comes to rules. You can still go today and buy at the age of twelve a pack of cigarettes and a bottle of KEO from a kiosk and no one would ask for ID. So, then it was exactly the same. It does help if your friends' parents own clubs and hotels. So, I can say, "Damn you Tom Cruise". Because I watched Cocktail *for the first time and after that I wanted to be a bartender. That's how it all started. I thought I was like really cool. My friend was DJing at a club and had all the DJing equipment at home. I kept trying and whatever. Started playing in clubs at the age of seventeen and I was working as a bartender in hotels. Summer jobs. Summer jobs became weekend jobs for extra cash, which my dad was never happy about. It wasn't something he was happy for me to do, but it just happened.*

I went up one summer to Napa and I just stayed up there and ended up being five seasons there. I worked up there while I was studying. In Ayia Napa it felt weird when they actually told me not to use my name Hamees, "Say your name is Harry and try to pretend you're English-Cypriot. Nobody will ever ask you. For work visas and stuff."

Being a citizen of a third-world country, Hamees was not legally permitted to work, despite having lived on the island for most of his life. As most non-Europeans, his family had to renew their 'Pink Slip' visa annually to legalise their 'temporary residence'. This permitted them to live on the island for the coming year though not engage in employment.

'So, I was going up and back. Graduated, spent another two seasons up there, well a season and a half and then decided to come back to Nicosia because I was tired of that kind of industry there. Found a job in a restaurant here. Then one day I woke up and I was like, I'm doing the same thing over and over again every day. No life, fifteen hour a day of work.

My dad wanted us (my family) to have something that when we needed it we could use to do other stuff. If we wanted to study abroad, wanted to do something with our life. Give yourself an identity rather than not having been, not to be limited... There is no way I could travel to the U.S with a Lebanese passport eas-

ily, especially nowadays. It's a whole different ball game. The day that I got the Cypriot passport, it felt good. I was… you know when you do that shimmy dance by yourself? It was like all the stress that I didn't really think about, it all left. Having the passport enabled me to travel wherever I wanted to and do what I wanted to, rather than apply for a visa. Have to get permission and deal with a person who just woke up late in the morning and whatever, taken his kids to school or something, got upset by somebody, given the bird while he's driving or that someone just looked at him in a bad way and then my fate is in his hands to give me an acceptance to go somewhere or not. It's just people. The world isn't evil, the people are. The waiting… that whole thing just went away. I was close to being cocky. Whenever someone would ask, "D'you you have a Work Visa?" I would answer, "No I have my passport." And shake it around. It was the only time I felt like I can do what I liked.

I realise it's so ridiculous. It's a stupid piece of paper that can allow you to do something or disallow you to do something else. Change where are you from and what your identity is. I'm still the same person. I'm still the same simple person but what you see is what you get.

I also wanted to help people, something I always wanted to do. I wanted to work with people but not necessarily for events and parties. Just to see a different perspective on people's needs rather than do a wedding for somebody. There are other needs that you can fill.'

Hamees got involved with various NGOs who were assisting refugees and migrants residing on the island. As a speaker of Arabic, English and Greek, his job mainly consisted of translating. Seemed basic enough? But part of the job as the ear and mouth between interlocutors was to remain just that, ears and mouth, because there was a danger of allowing words to travel along his nerves and into his heart, allowing the pain of others to haunt his quiet moments, his moments alone.

'You have sympathy for things and then you start feeling it first because you have become sympathetic to people. So, you start feeling the story as they're telling it. At first, you'll be like you hear the stories of people, what they went through their life. A life changing experience, you can say. Then you become numb without even realising you become numb to the stories. And the reason is because the more you hear it, at first you feel as though you're living it with them. Sometimes and afterwards, you just have to switch yourself off. With a few places I work with, I try not to remember people's names. I try to be the voice of the person that is talking and the person that needs the help. So, when I leave and they go, "Do you remember going to that place?" I'm like, "No." and I know without realising, I shut myself off because I don't want to give that person a name in their story. That's how I protect myself. I need to.

At first, when I didn't have this protection, the stories did affect me a lot. I was unemployed at the time and I turned around and said, "OK there's no point in me doing that because I know people who don't do a thing. I won't put myself in their shoes but I'll let myself go." In the sense I'll limit myself to their stories and lifestyles and follow that. "OK, there's no need for me to get a job. I'll go off and sign on unemployment." I said I'll do it but I never did. My mindset at the time was, "Why should I do that when they can't do that?" or, "Why should I do that when that person can't be doing that?" I could say I went into...I won't say depression but I'd go home and sleep a lot. I'd switch off from the world. I stopped socialising with people because it's all bullshit. Whatever's happening, it's not real. They don't know what's really happening out there. When you hear stories of certain people in there. That's not real. What we are doing now and what they're going through, hearing a story of a kid on a boat for ten hours going across from Turkey to Cyprus and the waves are ten metres high, they're covered in water… you know what I mean? And then you see like OK, what's the point in going to a café and doing stuff with people? It got me a little bit depressed, I could say. Then one day I had to snap out of it. I had to say, "Dude, just get your finger out. They are living theirs so you gotta live your life." And you can't listen to all the stories. This is what I realised afterwards. Yeah, you just can't keep on absorbing things. You just want to hear it and move on, hear it and move on.

I don't want to say I now "belong to Cyprus", but I can say "I belong to the world". This is what I have understood through the stories I recount daily and through the people that pass through the Cypriot border. Belonging somewhere, it is all out of our hands, it is all ludicrous. Noone can say, "Oh look, he has a beard. He must be a terrorist because he has a Lebanese passport" and then not give me permission. No. With this passport, I create my own reality.

People are people, don't let their stupidity create your reality. Keep going forward to it.'

I am EKA

Cyprus is like my home yes.
Not like, it IS my home.

'I always say, after life I die and I straight got to Heaven because in life I already been in Hell.'

Georgia. A country nestled between Russia (to the north), Turkey and Armenia (to the south), Azerbaijan (southeast) and the Black Sea (west). It is set as a bridge between Western Asia and Eastern Europe. In the nineteenth century, parts of its kingdom founded strong allegiances with Russia. In 1921, after the Red Army's invasion of Georgia, also known as the Soviet-Georgian War, Soviet forces claimed Georgia as their own, the Georgian Soviet Socialist Republic, and eventually established complete control in 1924.

'My mother and father were very wise people. My dad was an engineer and he was putting up the buildings. My mother was an accountant. Her aunt has a fabric (factory) which was making the wool. She had thirty-two persons under her. She was the boss, I had beautiful life. We had six sister. We go holidays. It was fantastic life. My grandma was working at home. Even the government was helping us. They gave five-bedroom house because my dad and mum have many kids but all these things disappear. We lost everything when the war happened.'

Georgia, as so many other ex-Soviet States, gained its independence in 1991. During this period, or shortly afterwards, various regions within the territory of Georgia pushed for secession. The president, Zviad Gamsakhurdia, armed with a nationalistic tempo, asserted the capital's jurisdiction over the independence-seeking territories and, in a dictator-like fashion, opted for executions of subjects opposing his goals. In a violent coup, the first president was deposed and forced to seek asylum in Chechnya, whilst the country dissolved into a civil war lasting until 1995. The conclusion was the de facto annexation of Abkhazia and South Ossetia, but not before a great many lives were lost to the conflict.

'You waking next morning. You hear these booms. You hear screaming and you moving with your slippers in winter time. Through snow we walk. Terrible winter time. You trying to get into these boats and people are throwing each other down able to reach there. It's like hell for me that moment. I swear that moment. Even now I take therapy because of that. It's terrible memory for me. This is what happened in Georgia.

From that time I never remember anything good happen. It was always sickness, always fighting, screaming and shouting. I remember I had to sew my own shoes to get to school. I never have enough books. I never have enough. I remember we became so nervous. We was hating each other but, I don't know, we survived.

I was lucky with my Grandma, from my mother's side. She was living on the other side of Georgia. She had farm and land. My father start from zero but he said he didn't know how to work with fields. They were struggling. They don't know how to take care of animals. There was nothing you know. They, government, was giving one bread, one kilo sugar and one litre oil just to survive. I have five sisters. It was so hard and I was very young. I remember we were going nine hundred times to the fridge and wardrobes to see if there was something to eat. I remember the place where I was going to pick up this stuff. People was killing each other there. We was waking midnight just to stay in the queue. It was even luck if you get it. When they were saying, "...people who have diabetes they must be first." You know other people tried to jump. There was people coming outside and you have to wake them up. They were losing their mind. This was happening in 1992. When we lost Abkhazia. I was part of that land.

I remember my Grandma was very rude to my mother. Saying she don't know anything. After my mother was hating herself and she was hitting and punishing herself. And my mother become sick. She got pneumonia because of no food. We were thinking that she would die. I remember going to the hospital and screaming to the doctors. They don't want to touch my mother because we don't have money. Imagine that! My mother was dying bleeding and they don't want to touch my mother. They were asking if we have money. I remember telling them, "Do you need my organs? Take my organs to heal my Mum!" It's a terrible thing. It not just happen only with me. It happened to half of the Georgians. It became a lot of corruption. Stealing, killing, drugs.

Being there, to be honest was not easy. I seen how pig eat human bodies. I have seen how animals, wolves and dogs, I've seen when they got shot and how blood flashes your face. I have walked the mountains without shoes in the winter. It was like that. All these things I have passed when I was nine.

My elder sister got problems psychologically because the stupid Russian soldiers. Maybe the Georgians was doing the same during the war, I don't know I don't trust none of them because they all tried to kill us. They tried to rape my sister. But my mother stand in front of them and don't let. I remember how they slapped my mother. My mother fainted, fall on floor. I thought she dead. I remember these two soldiers grab my sister. I don't know what happened. I believed it was God saving us. Somebody start shooting somewhere nearby and they take attention there so they put my sister down. From this time my sister…she had problems, nightmares. But thank God now she's OK.

Now, when bad things happen, some evil, they say this happen because of Georgians. My nature, the people in my age, they all destroy and what they learn? How to steal. They are robbers, they are…corrupt. But who to blame? My people? No. I want to ask the people accusing why don't you ask them why you do this? Because we grow just to survive. And, of course, it is the political government. Not because I want to be a person who do something bad. But we have no choice.

Well, because of the situation a lot of people left to Turkey, to different countries. One my aunts go to Greece and she managed to work there. When I grow I call her and say, "Please we need help. We need to survive. Could you help us to find any kind of work? I can come there and work, so I can take care of my family." She start preparing but it takes so long. It's very difficult to fix this time the Visa in Georgia and they were not giving you. Instead, you had to hide under buses or suitcase to get out. People were inside in the suitcase just to pass the borders. And many people died!

I had this experience my own self. I apply to go to Greece from woman, she like Mafia. 3,500 Euro they took. Not U.S. They took from my hands. Until now I'm looking for this woman and I couldn't find. I hear the police catch her. I don't think so because there is a lot of people still looking for her. It's like contraband. She cheated not only me but a lot of people. Anyway, instead of Greece, they, her group, take me from Georgia to Turkey and then to another Turkey here. They call this Turkey. I came as illegal. I thought these people would fix visa for me but it was lie. They took my passport. When I asked them to give me my passport they scare me and tell me, "If you don't want to die, you have to shut up."

So, I was scared and I was praying all the time, "Just God, don't kill me!" because I was not worrying about myself. I was worrying about my mother and my family because I know they were gonna die. But you know I came here. We come from Turkey side to this side by boat. Then there was trouble, police see them and they become scared. So, they throw me, us, inside in the sea. By swimming we came somewhere, we didn't know where, and from this we had to, you know like soldiers, to go down under the grass, hide and crawl. After they find us, or others find us and take us inside of a car so small–we were twenty person–I couldn't breathe inside. They left us somewhere in Limassol.

I arrive in 2006. I came here in Cyprus and I contact finally person that I have to contact. One person give me number on paper and I call this number. Where even now I'm not speaking maybe the good language that is English but at this time I knew some language.

In the first two weeks, I stay with one Georgian family, which was really disgusting people. I was sleeping on the floor. No bed. Even to take shower I had to ask them. I was hungry and I always remember the corner of Debenhams near where I stay. Coming down Debenhams and buying one apple. A piece of bread at 35 cent at that time. I had 100 US dollars in my pocket that Cypriot government give me as asylum seeker and I lived exactly one month with that money. And these idiot people, was asking me to give them money for electricity, for water, for food even I was not using so much. Even when I was going to wash they were knocking on the doors quickly, so I would not use so much water. I was twenty-three years old. After two days it was my birthday. Yeah, I never ever forget that, but I feel so blessed. I suffer. I had so much pain but you know I managed.

I was study midwife in Georgia but I couldn't manage to finish. I have some experience. My first work was as masseuse and physiotherapist. I had very good work. People was very happy there. After two weeks I start. At this time I had no Visa but I manage to work four years there. But in the end, I got very tired. It was very hard work. I got my sinus problem and I had to stop. After that it was very hard to find work without documents.

I was working as housekeeper. I was helping old people. Always with Cypriots. Also with who was working with the U.N. and I really want to thank these people. They helped a lot. They support me a lot and they was giving me work. And you know I don't know how but, maybe because of my honesty or my hard work. It's like a miracle. Even I have people from America, they just help me and lending me money and I'm thinking, how this happened? Because even my own family can't do this. Even your own people.

One time it was an old Cypriot woman I work for. No, not old. Around sixty years old who got a restaurant. I was working really hard. I remember kneeling down and crying because of pain, my neck and this. She was paying five Euros. It was so painful for me, I remember my hands was bleeding because of cleaning, cooking, sweating. I tell you I was screaming. One day when she come up, I decided to talk to her. I was scared maybe I was going to lose my work and will be back to my country but, you know, I was not care any more. I was leaving everything to God. Something help me, you know. She said, "OK, I'm sorry. I didn't know that you suffered so much." I know it's very hard from what happened between Turkey and Cyprus. They have same experience when I explain my life from my childhood, I could see her face she was sad about it and I think she understand me and she became sensitive to that. But after that I not stay. I couldn't. My character is like that. When I feel pain somewhere, I have to leave from there. I'm suffering. Even if they support me I can't, I have to leave.

So many times, I stay hungry because I don't have money because of no work, but also because I couldn't stay there I because I see they racist. You know, like they treat you like stupid person because you do this job but well, you have no power. You have no documents. You are not legal here. You just accept being slave.

I had to clean bathrooms, toilets, even I was brushing the roads. I was cleaning the school, the streets just to survive. I was thinking, "If you don't try this, you don't go out there." Maybe I was shy but I was crying. I was suffering. I knew people was coming. I was hiding my face. It was my pain.

Shame.

It doesn't matter, I overcame this problem.

After four years, I finally received Asylum Seeker status. I was blessed. I work another four to five years with that. After that I got married. I met one guy, he European, who we fall in love with each other. He tried to help me, even though it was so quick to marry but you know we fit each other, we have similar things. Seven years we are now together.

When I go back, it's just pain. Terrible pain. Memories. Terrible memories. I always think that I want this country to be OK even with Russian or without Russian. I don't know why we have to separate from Russian? People think Europe is more free and more freedom. It is but if I look back in my childhood, it was fantastic. We have work. I don't know what Russian was doing wrong. They said we don't have freedom. Maybe they were right, we don't have freedom. We don't have time for knowledge and grow more and do more. But I really don't know what happened. If it not happened, sure I would not be here. I would be like Russians coming and going like tourists. But now I'm here because of what's happened after Independence. And when Russian soldiers come back.

All I can say is, thanks to Cyprus government. Thanks to Cyprus people. I even don't imagine, I can't even imagine leave for another country. It's became like my soul. Like my home. My survivor. This land. Every morning I sleep and I wake up, I bless this island because this island saved my family and saved me and my own life. Cyprus is like my home, yes. Not like, it IS my home. I think I belong to be here. I don't want to go elsewhere. I want to fix my life here. I want to invest my life here and I want to be here. I don't even want to imagine I have to leave from Cyprus. It would kill me. I don't make any problem, any trouble. I think in the end they will accept me here.'

What is a Cypriot?

'Bastards'

'Warm Mediterranean people'

'In my mind and in my heart, Cyprus is like being in one bubble. But being a Cypriot is to be very laid-back, lazy, isolated and narrow-minded. Sort of isolated.'

'Being a Cypriot is, like what does it actually mean? It's a word that means a whole bunch of sentences. Somebody from Cyprus. Soaked a bit of the culture in, the environment in who's living here. But I change the definition, what it means and so do you.'

'Cypriot is close to me here. Because he like food. Me too, I like food. They are Arabic in their way. We share something.'

'It's not me telling the story of the Cypriots. It's me telling my story with Cypriots.'

'What I would want Cypriot to be is a group of people with an open mind but still be aware of what is going on, be willing to communicate and be open to new experiences and new people, less judgmental of people of darker ethnicity as well. What connects these people is the island. The fact that we all live here.'

'A people that are very nationalistic, at times. Genetically speaking a very interesting mix, that not many locals know of. There was a Cypriot geneticist who was looking into the genetic make-up of Cypriot DNA and seeing the percentages of it. And there was a big portion of it that was actually Italian. Because Cyprus used to be a Venetian colony, more so than Greek. Syrian as well. That really opened up my mind, wow this place is very diverse but also surprisingly not very open to those races. They still see Greece as the big brother. But I think that Cyprus can own its difference. It is fine that we are not fully Greek, that is what makes us so different. That is why I am proud of my Cypriot heritage. We are an island between three continents. It makes sense. Cyprus then can be defined as mixed in a beautiful way, so diverse, so many differences, we need to own that and we need to celebrate that more. I think we don't celebrate that enough.'

'You cannot generalise them, you cannot because you have some very good people and bad guys in every society.'

'To me, a Cypriot is not someone who has a Cypriot passport or nationality but is someone who is actually part of the Cypriot culture and heritage. Who definitely speaks Greek, who can probably say which village their parents were born in, who come from Famagusta, which they say is half of them. To me, an important part of being Cypriot is having that background. The cultural background.'

'As long as people show their willingness to integrate, they will accept them. It takes a lot of time and effort. I show I want to be part of the culture here. This is what I feel to be. They feel more comfortable calling me a Cypriot. If they are talking to a foreigner who is sitting there, who doesn't want to learn Greek, he just

wants to live as he wants to live. He's constantly whining about the country then yeah it's like, "What the fuck are you doing? Why do you want to be Cypriot? Get out. Go somewhere else." If you've always got something else to talk about this place and not trying to make it a better place, then what are you doing? Clearly, you shouldn't be here, and you should go back to yours.'

'The Cypriot is Arab people speaking Greek.'

'Cypriot citizen is a person who has acquired Cypriot citizenship either from birth or from seven years of presence when you are entitled to apply for citizenship, but this does not oblige the government that just because you stayed here for seven years they have to give it to you. And, of course, now we have something, which personally I disagree, if you invest 2 million 500, you get the citizenship. I disagree, it is like selling my nationality.'

'My answer would be very different in the 80s and now. In the 80s I will explain to you and what I feel now, I think Cypriots have made a very big jump in a very short time. They have changed a lot. Some things for the best, some things not. But I feel like there has been this huge jump. I feel I am in a different country now than in those years. But still I see the racism. Lots of racism.'

'A complete Jew.'

'I think the older Cypriots, the generation of the grown-up, are very kind, warm-hearted, welcoming, open-minded. I think they are very warm people. They welcome you in. New generation here is more about brands and more selfish, I think they are more looking into themselves. I think this is basically very different. I see the difference between the generations, I know a lot of

older people, a few, and I know a few young kids, and I see them on the street and I see what they are doing, I think they are very different. I think they are more spoiled and more who have fun. But, really, they are very good people. In general. It is very easy to be here. Simple life.'

Acknowledgements

There are so many people I owe the writing of this book to but I will try to keep it to just this one page.

First of all, I would like to thank the beautiful voices that offered their stories for this collection. You have no idea how much your stories have impacted me. In the way I view the world, in the choices I make. Thank you for your honesty and your time, for your patience even when you felt you were finished but the questions kept coming. You are Cyprus and you have taught me what being means.

Next, are the people who supported the project along the way. Kate Shylo, you truly are one of the most genuine people out there with a true passion for change. Without you, I would not have been so fortunate to hear some of the stories in this collection. How can I ever thank you enough? Argyri Loizou, when most people were enjoying their frapes and lounging by the beach, you were so kind enough to put in hours and hours and hours of labour into transcribing some of these stories. For your sweat and the pain that having to listen to my voice over and over again must have caused you, I truly am sorry, and I want to send you so much gratitude and love. Thank you. Melissa Chedid from Caritas, thank you for putting me in touch with so many of the people that

I was was genuinely appreciated. Antonella Mantovani and Benito Mantovani, thank you both for opening your doors and your contacts for me. Your warmth was infectious.

To Angela Petrou. You were there when I thought I should give up, when I was exhausted and when I was lost. And you continue to be. How am I so fortunate to have such a loving and compassionate friend?

To my publishers, Haris and Katerina. Without your passion for the cause, none of this would have been possible. Thank you for your heart, thank you for your support, and thank you for taking a chance on me. From that first day I walked into your office, I have truly felt supported by such a great team. Thank you.

To my family, I have to apologise for pushing your patience sometimes to extremes. Those days when you hardly saw me, the long nights with the lights coming from the bedroom door. To my grandparents, and my grandfather in particular, whose own stories inspired this one. Watching you devote afternoons writing about what you witnessed on the island, organically led to my own curiosity. You inspire me to not become a mere 'banka' pushed along by the breeze. I love you all.

A special thank you to James Mackay. From a professor to a mentor to someone I can call a friend. Over the years you have pressed me beyond what I thought were my limits. This project would have literally never existed if it were not for you. You pushed a somewhat benign idea for a small article to grow into something so much greater. I really cannot thank you enough. You have changed me in more ways than I thought were possible walking into that Shakespeare class, accidentally, all those years ago.

Finally, I would like to dedicate this book to my brother. Santi, I cannot offer you a world free of hate and hurt, even though I would like to. But I can offer you some advice. Listen, Santi, listen to the stories around you. And ask, keep asking, so that even the quietest of stories can become the voices that move you.

I am ANNETTA BENZAR

Annetta Benzar is a King's College London English graduate with an interest in migration, women's studies and trauma. She is the founder of iPoets, a platform for young writers to share their creative work, as well as Pe'Ta, a monthly Open Mic located in the town of Larnaca. This is her first book.